Science,
Technology
and
China's Drive for Modernization

HOOVER INTERNATIONAL STUDIES
Richard F. Staar, director

THE PANAMA CANAL CONTROVERSY
Paul B. Ryan

THE IMPERIALIST REVOLUTIONARIES
Hugh Seton-Watson

SOUTH AFRICA: WAR, REVOLUTION, OR PEACE?
L. H. Gann and Peter Duignan

TWO CHINESE STATES
Ramon Myers, editor

THE CLOUDED LENS: PERSIAN GULF SECURITY
James Noyes

SOVIET STRATEGY FOR NUCLEAR WAR
Joseph Douglass, Jr., and Amoretta Hoeber

SCIENCE, TECHNOLOGY AND CHINA'S DRIVE FOR MODERNIZATION
Richard P. Suttmeier

Science, Technology and China's Drive for Modernization

RICHARD P. SUTTMEIER

HOOVER INSTITUTION PRESS
Stanford University, Stanford, California

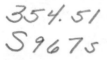
*The Hoover Institution on War, Revolution and Peace, founded at
Stanford University in 1919 by the late President Herbert Hoover,
is an interdisciplinary research center for advanced study on
domestic and international affairs in the twentieth century. The views
expressed in its publications are entirely those of the authors
and do not necessarily reflect the views of the staff, officers,
or Board of Overseers of the Hoover Institution.*

Hoover Institution Publication 223

Contents

Tables   *vii*

Editor's Foreword   *ix*

Preface   *xi*

Chapters

ONE   The Roots of a New Science Policy   *1*

TWO   Organization and Planning   *18*

THREE   Professional Life and Research Administration   *34*

FOUR   Manpower and Expenditures   *51*

FIVE   International Relations   *67*

SIX   The Politics of Chinese Science
and Sino-American Relations   *82*

Appendixes

ONE   Agreements Between the Governments of the United States
and the People's Republic of China on Cooperation in
Science and Technology   *95*

TWO   China's New Invention Law   *104*

Notes   *109*

Index   *117*

Tables

1 Technical Personnel, 1967   *53*
2 College Graduates, 1976–85   *55*
3 Growth in Demand for Engineers   *61*
4 Research and Development Expenditures
     by Major Categories, 1973   *63*
5 Science and Technology Budget, 1965   *64*

Editor's Foreword

It is fairly well known that since the mid 1960s, the leaders of the People's Republic of China have had different opinions regarding the direction in which science and technology should be developed. Until the death of Mao Zedong, scientific and technological organizations experienced considerable upheaval, and consequently the state of science and technology within China continued to decline compared with that of Japan and the West.

After the death of Mao and the emergence of new leaders, a reassessment of scientific and technological capabilities found them to be woefully inadequate. The new leaders decided to make a major commitment and build up organizations necessary to increase both scientific manpower and research facilities for development of science and technology.

To this end, the new leaders convened conferences, reorganized governmental administration, and signed new scientific and technological agreements with foreign countries in rapid sequence. The aims of the last activity are to train Chinese students and researchers abroad and to import the most advanced science and technology available in the West.

Professor Richard Suttmeier's study discusses these recent developments, but it also does something more. China's bid for modern technology came at a time when its leaders had embarked on a new foreign policy. This policy called for resumption of normal diplomatic relations with Japan and the United States and development of closer ties with Western countries. Of course, all these plans have been implemented, including expanded trade and the exchange of personnel and ideas.

How should the United States respond to China's demands for the most advanced science and technology within the context of this new foreign policy? How can the United States properly supervise the export to the People's Republic of China of its most advanced scientific knowledge? Or should it? These and other relevant questions are probed in depth by this study. Easy answers are not to be found, as the reader will quickly realize.

But unless these questions are posed and until we realize the implications of the dramatic change now occurring in China because of the new commitment to develop science and technology, we cannot begin to understand and influence the foreign policy we must fashion in the 1980s.

RICHARD F. STAAR
Director of International Studies
Hoover Institution

Preface

◆—◆

When I agreed to write this short monograph for the Hoover Institution Press in September 1977 it had been about one year since Mao Zedong had died and less than one year since the radical Gang of Four had been purged. Deng Xiaoping had just been reinstated to positions of authority. A survey of events in China indicated that significant changes in policy were occurring. However, it was difficult at that time to anticipate the speed with which new policies, particularly in science and technology, would be announced and implemented. Subsequent events, of course, indicated a very rapid movement away from the politics and policies that had characterized China throughout much of the period since 1966.

In writing the book, therefore, I always felt that I was in the precarious position of running hard to catch up with events. The submission of the manuscript was delayed several times beyond the date agreed on in order to include significant new developments. The Hoover Institution Press showed patience and understanding with these delays.

My appreciation of China's policies for science and technology and its problems of scientific development was deepened significantly as a result of a trip to China in May 1978 as a member of the Pure and Applied Chemistry Delegation sponsored by the Committee on Scholarly Communication with the People's Republic of China (CSCPRC). The delegation was the first to visit China after the important National Science Conference in March 1978. I am grateful to the CSCPRC for affording me that opportunity and to the distinguished chemists who were part of the delegation and who helped me see China's problems of science and technology through the eyes of working scientists and engineers. Thanks go also to our Chinese hosts, who helped me better understand Chinese perspectives on scientific development.

I also owe a debt of gratitude to Jon Sigurdson, director of the Research Policy Program at the University of Lund, Sweden, for sharing with me his manuscript on Chinese science and technology, for calling my attention to important documents, and for stimulating my thinking about Chinese scientific manpower and research and development expenditures. Ms. Leslie Evans rendered extraordinary services in typing the manuscript. Thanks go also to John Ellis for his skillful preparation of the index.

Chapter One

◆—◆—◆

The Roots of a New Science Policy

Since the end of 1976, a major change in policy for the development of science and technology has occurred in the People's Republic of China. Throughout the PRC's thirty years, its leaders have shown a commitment to science and technology in Chinese development. However, the approaches taken in support of science and technology have varied considerably over time. This variation derived from a lack of consensus among the leaders over the appropriate strategy for scientific and technological development; the relation between scientific and technological development, on the one hand, and revolutionary social change, on the other; and the ordering of techno-economic and sociopolitical values.

Events since January 1975 have developed in such a way that it now appears that a fairly stable consensus on policy for science and technology has emerged. In January 1975, at the Fourth National People's Congress, Premier Zhou Enlai advanced the doctrine of the "four modernizations," which would commit China to the goals of the comprehensive modernization of agriculture, industry, national defense, and science and technology by the year 2000. During the 22 months following Premier Zhou's statement, an intense struggle over political succession involved science and technology in unusual ways. Consensus on the means and ends of the four modernizations was impossible. But the October 1976 purge of the more radical leaders who have become known as the Gang of Four and the reemergence of Deng Xiaoping as the leading proponent of the four modernizations finally helped to create the elusive consensus. The consensus not only concerned the desirability of the goal of the four modernizations, it also included a belief that the modernization of science and technology is crucial to achieving the other three ends.

Science and technology policy, in short, has become a high-priority policy area in China. That it has become so is both fascinating and problematic for reasons pertaining both to the future and to the past. For the future, the content and the success of China's policies on science and technology will influence the kind of society China will be in the year 2000. Such is the view of present Chinese leaders, as well as of foreign observers.

The commitment to science and technology is fascinating for historical reasons as well. At the risk of a slight overstatement, one can argue that science and technology have been thorns in the sides of Chinese modernizers since the middle of the nineteenth century. The role of science and technology was an important cultural and social issue in precommunist China that was never fully resolved. In spite of new approaches to science, technology, and society in the People's Republic, the status of science and technology remained problematic. The reasons for this are numerous; some of them are explored in this book.

The appearance of China's new policy has been curiously linked with the problems of political succession since 1972. Once the most serious problem of succession—the claims to legitimate power by the Gang of Four—was eliminated by the gang's purge, steps were begun to redirect China's science and technology in late 1976 and early 1977. A newer, more receptive attitude toward foreign technology was evident before the end of 1976, and in May 1977 Party Chairman Hua Guofeng issued instructions to accelerate the development of science and technology. In doing so, he cited Mao Zedong's 1964 remark that China's tasks are to promote the "three great revolutionary movements of class struggle, the struggle for production, and the struggle for scientific experiment." The pace quickened during the summer when the Chinese Academy of Science held a national work conference to explore the meaning and implications of the new line. By the end of the summer, the race to modernize science and technology became an enthusiastic run. Following the Eleventh Party Congress during the summer, the party's Central Committee issued a "Circular on Holding a National Science Conference," a conference scheduled for spring, 1978. The circular led to a preparatory meeting on September 25 attended by over two hundred party, government, and military leaders from both central and provincial organs. Provincial-level meetings to prepare for the national conference were subsequently held throughout the fall. An outline of the national program for developing the basic sciences was prepared at a national conference held in Beijing in October, attended by 1,200 scientists and administrators from all over the country. In addition, in October the State Council issued new policies for enrolling students in colleges and universities.

The flurry of activity during the latter part of 1977 and early 1978 culminated in the convening of the National Science Conference in March 1978. The conference was an occasion for paying tribute to many of the scientists, engineers, and innovators among the 6,000 participants. It was also an opportunity to unveil China's research priorities for the coming years, priorities that had been hammered out during the preceding twelve months. We know of these plans, known as the "Outline National Plan for the Development of Science and Technology, 1978–85 (Draft)," through a report made at the conference by Fang Yi, minister in charge of the Science and Technology Commission and a member of the communist party's Politburo.[1] Due to the importance of the report, it is worth quoting at length.

THE PLAN FOR SCIENTIFIC DEVELOPMENT

The broad objectives of the plan are (1) to reach "advanced world levels of the 1970's in a number of important branches of science and technology" in order to narrow "the gap [with the advanced countries] to about ten years" and lay "a solid foundation for catching up with or surpassing advanced world levels in all branches in the following 15 years"; (2) to "increase the number of professional research workers to 800,000"; (3) to "build a number of up-to-date centers" for research; and (4) to "complete a nationwide system of scientific and technological research."

The plan calls for comprehensive preparations for research in 27 "spheres," including natural resources, agriculture, industry, national defense, transport and communications, oceanography, environmental protection, medicine, finance and trade, culture, and education, "in addition to the two major departments of basic and technical sciences." Within these 27 spheres, 108 items of research have been selected as "key projects."

Eight "comprehensive scientific and technical spheres, important new technologies and pace-setting disciplines that have a bearing on the overall situation" were singled out for special prominence. These are—

1. *Agriculture*: Fang generally followed Hua Guofeng's speech to the National People's Congress (see below), but discussed the plans for agriculture in greater detail. He called for full-scale implementation of the Eight-Point Charter for Agriculture (soil, fertilizer, water conservancy, seeds, close planting, plant protection, field management, and improved farm tools) and for the use of scientific farming to increase agricultural output. Science and technology are to be applied to the areas of mechanization, soil improvement, soil and water conservancy, fertilizers, plant breeding, cultivation techniques, insecticides, and disease and pest prevention. Forestry, livestock management, fisheries, and agricultural sideline industries are also to benefit through science and technology.

2. *Energy*: In the area of oil production, Fang urged that China should use its resources rationally and "catch up with and surpass advanced world levels." He repeated the party's objective of "building of some ten more oilfields, each as big as Taching."

Coal production is to be mechanized. Scientific and technical work should emphasize "basic theory, mining technology, technical equipment and safety measures. At the same time research should be carried out in gasification, liquefaction and multi-purpose utilization of coal and new ways explored for the exploitation, transportation and utilization of different kinds of coal."

The chief research subjects in the power industry should be "the key technical problems in building large hydroelectric power stations and thermal power stations at pit mouths, large power grids and super-high-voltage power transmission lines" and the techniques involved "in building huge dams and giant power generating units."

Alternate sources of energy—atomic, solar, geothermal, wind, tidal —and energy conservation are also to be explored.

3. *Materials*: As key areas for research and technological development, Fang singled out metallurgy, intensified mining, multipurpose utilization, the exploitation and refining of copper, aluminum, nickel, cobalt, and rare earths, geological surveying, organic synthesis based on fossil fuels, catalysts, plastics, synthetic fibers, and automation in the petrochemical industry. China is to become one of the leading producers of titanium and vanadium and in general exploit its mineral resources fully and effectively.

4. *Computer Science and Technology*: Fang noted that "the electronic computer is developing in the following directions: giant computers, microcomputers, computer networks and intelligence simulation. The scientific and technical level, scope of production and extent of application of computers have become a conspicuous hallmark of the level of modernization of a country." Accordingly, China must rapidly solve problems relating to the industrial production of large-scale integrated circuits and must work on the technology of ultralarge-scale integrated circuits, peripheral equipment, software, applied mathematics, and the problem of computer applications. Efforts will also be made to popularize microcomputers and establish a number of computer networks and data bases. By 1985, China hopes to have "a comparatively advanced force in research in computer science and build a fair-sized modern computer industry." Key industries will use computers for process control and managment.

5. *Lasers*: Fang noted the application of lasers in material processing, precision measurement, remote ranging, holography, telecommunications, medicine, and seed breeding and the potential application in isotope separation, catalysis, information processing, and controlled fusion. For the future, Fang stated:

> We will study and develop laser physics, laser spectroscopy and non-linear optics in the next three years. We should solve a series of scientific and technical problems in optical communications, raise the level of routine lasers quickly and intensify our studies of detectors. We expect to make discoveries and creations in the next eight years in exploring new types of laser devices, developing new wave-lengths of lasers and studying new mechanisms of laser generation, making contributions in the application of lasers to studying the structure of matter. We plan to build experimental lines of optical communications and achieve big progress in studying such important projects of laser applications as separation of isotopes and laser-induced nuclear fusion. Laser technology should be popularized in all departments of the national economy and national defence.

6. *Space*: Again, Fang summarized the scientific and technological progress achieved in other countries as a result of the development of space technology. China's work in this field is to include space science, satellites and ground facilities for remote sensing and other applications, the building of modern space centers, and the development of launch vehicles and skylabs.

7. *High Energy Physics*: In 1972, the Academy of Sciences established a new institute for high energy physics. The plans for high energy physics, according to Fang, were as follows:

> We expect to build a modern high energy physics experimental base in ten years, completing a proton accelerator with a capacity of 30,000 million to 50,000 million electron volts in the first five years and a giant one with a still larger capacity in the second five years. Completion of this base will greatly narrow the gap between our high energy accelerators and advanced world levels and will stimulate the development of many branches of science and industrial technology.

Fang also called for increased training of researchers, more research on high energy physics and cosmic rays, practical application in industry, agriculture, and medicine, and greater integration between high energy physics and neighboring disciplines.

Work on a 50 BeV proton synchrotron has started in Beijing,[2] and China has sought and received advice and cooperation from the high energy physics communities in Europe and the United States.

8. *Genetic Engineering*: Fang noted that the techniques of genetic engineering could be used to "create new biological species to meet the needs of humanity" and would "open new vistas for momentous changes in agriculture, industry, medicine," and other fields. China "has a rather weak foundation" in this area. In the next three years, China should

"strengthen organization and coordination," construct improved research facilities, and conduct basic studies. Over the next eight years, this new technology should be applied to pharmacology and medicine and to plant breeding.

To achieve the goals of the Outline National Plan for the Development of Science and Technology, which in turn were linked to economic and defense objectives, major changes in the institutional setting for science and technology were initiated. Before discussing these in detail, let us first review the economic and political factors that form the immediate background of China's new science policy.

THE PROBLEMS OF PRODUCTION, EDUCATION, AND TECHNICAL MANPOWER

Ignoring politics for the moment, one can view China's new policies for science and technology as a rational, calculated response to problems militating against the realization of the four modernizations. The central economic problem confronting Chinese leaders in the early 1970s was the need to stimulate economic growth and to achieve economic modernization, including the establishment of reliable sources of innovation for production in agriculture and industry. Despite respectable economic performance for the twenty-odd years since 1949, Chinese leaders were clearly concerned that the economy was not moving sufficiently smoothly and rapidly. There is good reason to think that China's economy had reached the point where desired, major gains in productivity would come only from technological innovation. The two main sources of such innovation available to China were, and are, indigenous research and development and foreign technology. The changes in China's policy for science and technology were designed to strengthen the former and to take fuller advantage of the latter.

However, the quest for reliable sources of innovation called attention to other constraints. Perhaps the most significant was that of quality scientific manpower. Since the communists came to power, the leadership of China's scientific community has come from a cohort of scientists and engineers who were trained abroad or in China before 1949. Members of this group have occupied the key positions in research institutes and universities throughout the history of the People's Republic. However, as we shall see in chapter 3, they have also been central targets for ideological remolding and political manipulation of varying intensity over the years. The employment of this group has been an issue of controversy since the beginning of the Cultural Revolution.

As a consequence of the Cultural Revolution, research institutes and universities were subject to policies intended to make them more accessible and responsive to what were perceived to be the needs and interests of the masses. One result was to downplay expertise generally and the expertise of senior scientists in particular. However, the expertise of senior scientists, for both research and training, was among China's scarcest resources. In general, this resource was not wisely used either in research or in laying the foundation for future research through education and advanced training.

Independent of utilization policies was the simple fact of aging. In 1975, the mean age of the leading scientists of the Academy of Sciences (directors or deputy directors of institutes) was 67. Thus, by the early 1970s China faced the problem of the wasteful utilization of its senior scientists, a group that was dwindling because of old age and death.

A related constraint was in the educational system. Universities closed during the Cultural Revolution reopened only slowly. As they did, they reflected such mass, egalitarian reforms of the Cultural Revolution as admission based upon the recommendation of a candidate's workplace and a curriculum that was both shortened and emphasized knowledge of immediate usefulness and narrow specialization. The curriculum, in short, reflected views of science prevalent during the Cultural Revolution and the immediate post–Cultural Revolution period. It was not designed to produce a new generation of qualified scientists capable of doing research at world standards and of succeeding the aging senior scientists.

Concern over China's scientific manpower and the generational differences within the scientific community was reflected in discussions initiated by Deng Xiaoping in mid-1975 on the state of the sciences. In these discussions, China's scientists were divided into four generational groups: those trained abroad before 1949; those sent abroad after the Liberation; those trained in China after 1949; and those selected for training from among workers, peasants, and soldiers, primarily in accordance with the Cultural Revolution reforms. The discussions reflected skepticism about the long-term contributions that the last group might make and indicated that a large number of individuals from the third group had spent too much time detailed to production practice and manual labor at the grass roots to have the knowledge and experience necessary to perform high-quality research and development.[3]

The tone of Chinese discussions of these issues of science and education began to reflect a sense of crisis by the end of 1977.[4] China was beginning the drive for the four modernizations with a rather skewed distribution of manpower. Although the manpower question is discussed in somewhat greater detail in chapter 4, some of its characteristics can be noted here in rough qualitative terms.

The science and education policies of the PRC over the years did in fact have the consequence of recruiting a large number of people into science- and technology-related roles. One estimate of the number of scientific and technical personnel who had completed higher education as of mid-1975 is 1.3 million. Of this number, 575,000 were scientists, including agricultural and medical scientists, and the remaining 725,000 were engineers. Such estimates are fraught with difficulties, and as Leo A. Orleans, the author of this one pointed out, the 1.3 million figure masks an enormous variation in competence due to wide ranges of quality in the educational system and various changes in educational policies.[5]

Although educational policies created opportunities for large numbers, the curricular emphasis, as we have seen, was generally on practical work and not on advanced science and engineering. The result is that the bulk of China's technical manpower has a rather limited education, where "limited" means knowledge in depth of a narrowly defined topic or topics, but not the theoretical understanding needed to tackle new topics.

An exception to these generalizations has been the persistence throughout the history of the People's Republic of advanced training for a limited number within the institutes of the Academy of Sciences. The training has taken the form of research apprenticeships with one or more senior scientists. This system has produced younger scientists with knowledge of and research experience in topics of current world scientific interest, at least in some fields. There are indications, however, that even these apprentices lack the educational backgrounds to do creative basic science or to respond quickly in applied research and development to rapid changes in world science.[6]

Thus, there are strong indications that both quantitatively and qualitatively, China's manpower situation was anomalous, given the goals of the four modernizations. The normal distribution of manpower in an industrialized society is perhaps analogous to the shape of a pyramid. In the Chinese case, the base of the pyramid and the top, represented by those who benefited from "mass science" activities and those produced by the research apprenticeship system respectively, were in place. What the educational system did not produce, however, were those with strong scientific backgrounds who were capable of operating in the mid-range of the pyramid and performing those activities that in the West would be characterized as research and development in support of science-based technology. Such work, however, seems to be precisely what the goals of the modernization of agriculture, industry, and national defense require. In addition, the pyramid is seen by China's leaders as too small. In the words of Fang Yi: "It will never do for a vast country like ours to go without a professional contingent of *several million* people whose level is above that of university graduates. We must also have a mighty contingent of non-professional scientists and technicians." (Emphasis added.)[7] If Orleans's estimate of China's professional manpower in

1975 is correct, the manpower supply falls short of what the leaders think the country should have by at least a factor of two.

Chinese concerns about sources of innovation, manpower development, and more general scientific and technological progress are best understood in the context of the goals of economic development China has set for itself. Activities surrounding the four modernizations during the past few years have resulted in public documents detailing China's economic aspirations. A useful summary of these aspirations is found in Hua Guofeng's report on the work of the government given at the Fifth National People's Congress on February 26, 1978.[8] Hua's report contained the outlines of an ambitious ten-year economic development plan. The major sections of the plan were—

1. *Agriculture*: Strenuous efforts were to be made to increase grain production two to three times between 1978 and 1985 in the twelve large commodity-grain bases and on all state farms. Grain-deficient, low-yield areas were to attain self-sufficiency in two to three years. In addition, efforts would be made to increase cultivated acreage by land reclamation, soil improvement, and water control. Although much of this work was to be locally initiated and supported, the state would continue major water conservancy projects on the Yellow, Yangtze, Huai, Hai, Liao, and Pearl rivers.

   Efforts should be made to perfect the system of agro-scientific research and agro-technical popularization in order to insure linkages between advanced research and grass-roots problems. Targets for progress in the agro-technical area were seed improvement, farming methods, fertilizers, mechanization, and insecticides. Various sources of fertilizer should be "extensively explored," and "a big effort" should be made "to develop organic fertilizer and [make] proper use of chemical fertilizer." At least 85 percent of "all major processes of farmwork" were to be mechanized within ten years. Both fertilizers and insecticides should be made better and cheaper and designed to meet specific needs. The goal of these measures was to increase agricultural output by 4–5 percent per year between 1978 and 1985.

2. *Industry*: Increases in industrial output were targeted at 10 percent per year during the same period. According to Hua, the ten-year plan called for

   > the growth of light industry, which should turn out an abundance of first-rate, attractive and reasonably priced goods with a considerable increase in per capita consumption. Construction of an advanced heavy industry is envisaged, with the metallurgical, fuel, power and machine-building industries to be further developed through the adoption of new

techniques, with iron and steel, coal, crude oil and electricity in the world's front ranks in terms of output, and with much more developed petrochemical, electronics and other new industries. We will build transport and communications and postal and telecommunications networks big enough to meet growing industrial and agricultural needs, with most of our locomotives electrified or dieselized and with road, inland water and air transport and ocean shipping very much expanded. With the completion of an independent and fairly comprehensive industrial complex and economic system for the whole country, we shall in the main have built up a regional economic system in each of the six major regions, that is, the southwest, the northwest, the central south, the east, the north and northeast China, and turned our interior into a powerful, strategic rear base.

China's basic industries, such as mining, steel, power, fuel, and transportation, were to receive particular attention from the state. Some 120 large-scale projects were to be undertaken, including the building or completion of 10 iron and steel complexes, nine nonferrous metal complexes, 8 coal mines, 10 oil and gas fields, 30 power stations, 6 new trunk railways, and 5 key harbors. The completion of these would result in "14 fairly strong and fairly rationally located industrial bases." Hua's report also singled out the machine-building and petrochemical industries. The latter was to contribute to substantially increasing "the ratio of such petrochemically produced raw materials as chemical fibres and plastics to all raw materials used in light industry."

Hua's report also included a section on science, education, and culture. He noted in particular the expected contributions from science and technology in "rapidly transforming the weaker links in our economy, that is, fuel, electricity, raw and semi-finished materials industries, and transport and communications." Hua also anticipated the national research priorities (discussed above) announced at the National Science Conference in March 1978.

We must strive to develop new scientific techniques, set up nuclear power stations, launch different kinds of satellites, and step up research into laser theory and its application, attach importance to the research on genetic engineering and above all to research on integrated circuits and electronic computers and their widespread application. Full attention must be paid to theoretical research in the natural sciences, including such basic subjects as modern mathematics, high energy physics and molecular biology.

By the beginning of 1979 China's leaders realized that the goals expressed by Hua could not serve as realistic objectives for economic policy. It would be impossible to abide by the timetable contained in the speech and to develop simultaneously agriculture, light industry, and heavy industry. As a result, some of the objectives for heavy industry were set aside in the interest of agriculture and light industry. In spite of this retrenchment, Hua's speech should still be viewed as an important statement of longer-term aspirations, and hence as a source of influence on current policies for science and technology. The formulation of China's ambitious development plans was intended not only to spur economic growth, but also to achieve the kind of systemic change that we call economic modernization. The plans were a response to perceived problems in the economy of the early 1970s. China's leaders concluded that necessary conditions for the solution of these problems included greater reliance on foreign technology, the stimulation of domestic scientific and technological activities, and a major effort to overcome the serious distortions in the availability of technical manpower caused by the Cultural Revolution.

China's new policies for science and technology, however, were not merely the product of a rational, apolitical decision made in response to economic problems. They were also a function of a political process characterized by intense political conflict. Our understanding of the roots of current science policy would be incomplete without an examination of that process.

THE POLITICS OF SCIENCE AND POLITICAL SUCCESSION

For the student of Chinese science policy, the changes brought about following the death of Mao Zedong have been both predictable and surprising. The surprises are in the speed with which the changes occurred and in the degree of priority given to science and technology policy. On the other hand, Western observers and visitors to China could detect in the early 1970s that the number of constraints on future scientific and technological development and on the contributions of science and technology to economic growth were increasing. Major new policy initiatives were needed and could have been expected.

However, Chinese politics since the end of the Cultural Revolution had been exceedingly unstable. The Cultural Revolution not only produced new policies and institutional reforms, it also propelled individuals committed to the ideals of the Cultural Revolution into positions of leadership throughout the society. Initially many of these new leaders displaced pre-Cultural Revolution leaders, many of whom had been attacked, discredited, or purged. By the early 1970s, however, under the leadership of Premier Zhou Enlai, many of the older leaders were being rehabilitated and were reentering public life. Inevitably they become competitors with those whose fortunes had soared as a result of the Cultural Revolution. The latter were represented at the highest political levels by the group that came to be known as the Gang of Four, Mao's wife, Jiang Qing, Yao Wenyuan, Zhang Chunqiao, and Wang

Hongwen. The interests of the pre–Cultural Revolution technocratically oriented officials were represented by the late Premier Zhou Enlai, and after his reappearance in 1973, by Deng Xiaoping. The reinstatement of the pre–Cultural Revolution officials, not surprisingly, resulted in proposals for a return to many of the national development policies and institutional arrangements that were in force before the Cultural Revolution.

The politics of the early 1970s were, in short, marked by competing policies and competing partisans. These years were also marked by the gradual decline of Mao Zedong and the failing health of Zhou Enlai. Thus, the competition for power, positions, and policies was given a special edge by the participants' awareness of the imminence of the People's Republic's first political succession.

The relationship between science and technology policy and this larger political scene was rather obscure until fall, 1975. To be sure, the more radical aspects of Cultural Revolution policies toward science and technology were being tempered, and scientists and science administrators who had not been seen in public since the Cultural Revolution began to reappear in the early 1970s. In general, however, there were few new policy initiatives, and those that a careful observer might have noticed were counterbalanced by contradictory signals. Chinese politics and policy debates remained behind the veil of overt political campaigns, such as the "anti–Lin Biao, anti-Confucius" movement.

The involvement of science and technology policy in the succession struggle became evident in late 1975 and throughout 1976. As we have seen, at the Fourth National People's Congress in January 1975, Zhou Enlai enunciated the doctrine of the "four modernizations." Also in early 1975, Deng Xiaoping, who had been purged during the Cultural Revolution, was reinstated as vice-premier. In autumn, 1975, the Chinese press, which was largely under the influence of the Gang of Four, began to publish stout defenses of Cultural Revolution reforms in the field of education. These and other "newborn things" stemming from the Cultural Revolution were allegedly threatened by a "right-deviationist wind to reverse the verdicts" of the Cultural Revolution. By early 1976, the radical press was raising the alarm about the right-deviationist wind blowing in the fields of science and technology, as well as in education. As time went on, more was written about the specific properties of the wind, and its origins were traced to three major reports dealing with problems standing in the way of realizing the four modernizations. These reports were prepared in mid-1975 on instructions from Deng Xiaoping.

The first report, "Some Problems in Speeding Up Industrial Development," dealt with, among other things, questions of industrial management and foreign technology. On these issues, the report ran counter to many of the reforms inspired by the Cultural Revolution. It urged that factory management should be placed in the hands of professional managers with assistance from professional technical staffs instead of committees of party officials, workers, and technicians and that economic activities should be conducted according to rules and regulations under strong central control. It argued that the principle of self-reliance need not produce hostile attitudes toward or preclude the importation of foreign technology. The report recommended that in certain key industries arrangements should be made promptly to import technology to overcome production problems. It also called attention to the need to give indigenous science and technology a leading role in economic development.

The second report, "The Outline of the Summary Report on the Work of the Chinese Academy of Sciences," or "Outline Report," dealt more specifically with questions of science and technology. It was prepared by Hu Yaobang and Hu Qiaomu, two important nonscientist party officials purged during the Cultural Revolution after promising careers in youth work and culture-propaganda work, respectively.[9] The "Outline Report" was highly critical of the state of Chinese science and traced its shortcomings to Cultural Revolution reforms and the influence of the Gang of Four.

The third report was entitled "On the General Program for All Work of the Whole People and Whole Nation," or "General Program." It raised the question of the relation between class struggle and economic development, and reversed the interpretation of this relation that had prevailed since the Cultural Revolution by arguing that to stress the primacy of class struggle over policies for economic development was a serious ideological mistake.

From the point of view of the Gang of Four and their followers, these were threatening winds indeed. Not only did these reports oppose the policies and interpretations of the social role of science and technology held by the radicals, the power and positions held by the radicals were inseparable from the policies. The radicals, therefore, used their chief political resource, control over the press, to denounce the Deng-inspired documents repeatedly throughout 1976.

These press attacks continued, it should be noted, even after Deng Xiaoping was again removed from office in April, 1976, which suggests that the wind had a following more extensive than Deng and his immediate associates. The denunciations continued until the October 1976 purge of the gang.

Since the demise of the gang, more light has been shed on these debates over science and technology. Indeed, the extent of coverage given to the gang's allegedly pernicious influences on science and technology is itself curious and suggests a degree of intimacy between science policy and the political succession that was not obvious during 1975 and 1976.

According to accounts appearing since the downfall of the Gang of Four which are intended to expose the gang's crimes, the relation between science policy and high-level political struggle dates back to 1972 and initially concerned the question of basic research. The role of basic research in Communist China had always been somewhat ambiguous, but since the Cultural Revolution it had been particularly de-emphasized and neglected. In 1972, according to the post-gang accounts, the issue of basic research began to attract the attention of Mao Zedong and Zhou Enlai. Instrumental in raising their awareness was American physicist and Nobel laureate Yang Chenning. Yang had an audience with Mao and apparently helped Mao understand the importance of basic research in general and its importance for Chinese science at that time in particular. Reportedly, Mao instructed Zhou Enlai to pursue this matter, and Zhou in turn solicited the aid of one of China's most esteemed senior scientists, Zhou Peiyuan, then vice-president of Beijing University and vice-chairman of the Science and Technology Association. Zhou Peiyuan's assignment was to explore ways to strengthen basic research and, importantly, to strengthen teaching in this area in order to train people for work in basic science.

In consultation with the academic community in Beijing, Zhou Peiyuan prepared an article entitled "Some Views on Educational Revolution in the Science Faculties of Universities," which was published in *Guangming ribao* (Guangming Daily) in October 1972. The article emphasized the importance of basic research and of training in the basic sciences. It appeared at the time to be a first major step away from such Cultural Revolution antiprofessional themes as the need for research serving the immediate needs of production and the need to emphasize the creativity of the masses.

It now appears, however, that the article was in fact written in spring, 1972, and was to be published in *Renmin ribao* (People's Daily). Its publication there, however, allegedly was blocked by Gang of Four members Yao Wenyuan and Zhang Chunqiao. Yao and Zhang, writing in the Shanghai paper *Wenhui bao*, also attacked Zhou Peiyuan's article and the views it represented, arguing that the only basic theory needed for Chinese scientific development was Marxist philosophy.[10]

The attack on basic research reportedly was aimed at the proposed change in policy, but, more importantly, also at Zhou Enlai. It is now alleged that Zhang Chunqiao wished to become premier and therefore used the attack on Zhou Peiyuan's article to discredit the behind-the-scenes boss, Zhou Enlai.[11] If this interpretation is correct, the high political saliency of science policy in 1975–76 was a function of the linkage between the basic research question and the struggle for political power that characterized elite politics from the downfall of Lin Biao in autumn, 1971 to the downfall of the Gang of Four in autumn, 1976.

These revelations about the period since 1972 also contribute to our understanding of what was described above as contradictory signs about the direction of science policy in the 1970s. For while the radicals continued to promote their views of science and technology, the movement toward strengthening professionalism in science continued under the patronage of Premier Zhou and, according to reports in 1977, of Mao as well.

The movement to strengthen basic science continued into 1973. Mao reiterated his support for "basic science and revolutionary intellectuals,"[12] and Beijing University completed a report on education in the basic sciences in March. This report, "On Speeding Training of Scientific Research Personnel and Strengthening Theoretical Research in the Faculties of Science," was prepared for the then leading body in scientific and educational affairs, the Science and Education Group of the State Council. The report, however, allegedly was sabotaged by the Gang of Four.[13]

What is now portrayed as systematic resistance to the wishes of Mao and Zhou Enlai continued into 1974. Again Mao and Zhou supported efforts to strengthen basic science. Under Zhou's direction, a planning group for the development of basic science was established. When the group made a trip to investigate the state of science in Shanghai, the political base of the gang, its efforts were frustrated and criticized for attempting a plan for basic science divorced from production. Although the group did eventually produce a ten-year plan for developing basic science, the gang reportedly was able to impede its implementation.[14] Thus, even before the four modernizations doctrine presented at the Fourth National People's Congress explicitly focused on issues of science and technology, the press reports of 1977 give the impression that science and technology had been issues of major political significance since 1972.

It now appears that as early as the Fourth National People's Congress, those who championed the new policy felt that of the four modernizations, the modernization of science and technology was the key to the achievement of the other three. Following the congress, Hua Guofeng was given authority over scientific and technological work. Hua issued instructions not only to promote the scientific activities of the masses, but also to "give full play" to research institutes and to basic science.[15] By the end of the summer, 1975, the nonradical leaders gave unequivocal instructions to the Ministry of Education to "grasp basic sciences," and in early September the State Council convened a special meeting to hear an early version of the "Outline Report." Hua and others at this meeting called for the elimination of factionalism and for a change in science and technology policy.[16] The radicals must have perceived this report and the Deng-inspired documents discussed above as a challenge because they became the objects of the radicals' attacks throughout 1976. Again, however, according to reports in 1977, the attacks were not only against the policies, but against the men behind the policies as well. Not only were the media used, but the minutes of the State Council meeting were also obtained and selectively edited to highlight the "reverse the verdicts" speeches. Reportedly, the edited minutes were distributed to basic-level organizations for criticism.[17] In their attacks, the gang was aided by supporters in key positions in the Academy of Sciences in Beijing and in science policy bodies in the provinces, particularly in Shanghai, Liaoning, and Jilin.[18]

The discussion above clearly indicates that China's new science policy was long in coming and was a product of that most basic of political struggles—succession. The way that this struggle and the evolution of the policy have been reported since the beginning of 1977 warrants a few final reflections. The new leaders seemed eager not only to promote the new policy, but also to use this policy to discredit the Gang of Four.

At least two interpretations of the link between the promotion of the new policy and the denunciation of the gang are possible. One is that the new leaders were continuing the long-standing party tradition of promoting policy objectives by mobilizing the population against a specified common enemy. In this case, the enemy was the Gang of Four, which was portrayed as plotters against Zhou Enlai and unscrupulous schemers who used the symbolism of Maoism to frustrate the true intentions of Mao.

The other interpretation is that one of the functions of the way the new policy was presented was to buttress the legitimacy of the new leaders. The members of the Gang of Four did hold high party and government positions, and their incumbency had been more or less legitimated. Among the members of the gang was Mao's wife, and both the gang and the policies they represented had been more than casually associated with Mao in the eyes of many for a number of years. Futhermore, the number of supporters of the gang and its policies in different organizations and locations around the country was significant. In addition, the gang actively opposed Deng Xiaoping, who had twice been removed from office with Mao's acquiescence, if not at Mao's urging. Finally, the gang was removed from public life by an act of force. Given these factors, there was more than a prima facie case for questioning the legitimacy of the new leaders.

These interpretations are not mutually exclusive. If they are true, both China's new leaders and China's new policy—particularly since the policy resembles the pre–Cultural Revolution policy discredited earlier under Mao's leadership—needed legitimation. The new leadership spared no effort to provide it. A new volume of Mao's works that shows a different Mao from the Cultural Revolution Mao was published. More importantly for our purposes, extensive efforts were made to identify the new policy on science and technology with Mao and Zhou Enlai. This was done, as we have seen, by recounting the origins of the policy. As now told, the story of the events since 1972 consistently pictures the Gang of Four frustrating and sabotaging the wishes of Mao and Zhou regarding science and technology, in contrast to the loyal officials who later gained power, who labored to carry out the desires of the deceased chairman and premier.

The legitimation efforts were also approached in a spate of articles by and about well-known scientists. These articles typically celebrated professionalism in science—in keeping with the new policy—but also invariably mentioned Mao's and Zhou's interest in and concern for science and scientists.

China's new policy for science and technology and the plans for the modernization of agriculture, industry, and national defense are clearly directed toward rectifying some rather serious problems of national development. But they are also the product of a unique political history. As with any new policies, there was a need to build a consensus for their acceptance by presenting them in the context of the legitimating symbols of the political system. In this case, however, the building of legitimacy for the policies also involved the policies functioning to legitimize a new leadership.

The plans for the four modernizations are ambitious, and the political stakes high. As a result, heavy demands can be expected to be placed on China's institutions, including its system of science- and technology-related institutions. Before attempting to assess China's capacity to respond to these demands, it will be helpful to review some of the institutional changes in science and technology made since the beginning of 1977 and set these in a broader historical perspective.

Chapter Two

◆—◆—◆

Organization and Planning

The policy initiatives following Hua Guofeng's May 1977 statement on fostering scientific development were summarized in December by Fang Yi. Fang was by that time the highest political leader responsible for scientific and technological development. By early 1979, he was minister in charge of the new Science and Technology Commission, a vice-president of the Chinese Academy of Sciences, a member of the Politburo, and a vice-premier. Thus, he combined in ways unusual for any country high political position and direct responsibility for science and technology. Fang came to these positions with a career background in economic planning and foreign trade and hence could be expected to be a strong advocate of expanded international scientific and technological relations.

Fang's December report to the Chinese People's Political Consultative Conference in effect catalogued a twelve-point program for institutional reform.[1] According to Fang, the party's new policy involved—

1. *Science and technology*: The reestablishment of a state scientific and technological commission to "take charge of overall planning, coordination, organization and administration of the country's scientific and technological work." Administrative agencies concerned with science and technology at the provincial, municipal, and autonomous-region levels were to be strengthened;

2. *Research*: The reorganization of leadership in research institutes and universities. In particular, "the Party Central Committee has approved that all scientific research institutions must practice the system of directors assuming responsibility under the leadership of the Party committees";

3. *Long-term planning*: The reintroduction of long-term national planning in science and technology and in education;

4. *Responsibilities*: The redefinition of the responsibilities of central and local authorities. Some scientific research institutions "which should not have been disbanded" either had been or were being restored;

5. *Achievements*: The recognition of scientists and technologists for outstanding achievements. Titles were being restored; work assignments of technical personnel were being reviewed, and unsuitable personnel assignments rectified;

6. *Academics*: The holding of academic conferences in the spirit of "letting 100 flowers bloom" in order to stimulate academic communication and "enliven academic studies." The activities of the Science and Technology Association and of academic societies had resumed;

7. *Education*: College and university enrollments based upon academic achievement. "Spare-time education, including vocational studies through radio and television," were to be further developed;

8. *Textbooks*: The preparation, under the leadership of the Ministry of Education, of standard textbooks incorporating the latest scientific and technical knowledge;

9. *Cooperation*: Without sacrificing the principles of independence and self-reliance, the encouragement of efforts "to learn advanced science and technology from foreign countries, actively enhance international academic exchanges and master . . . what is the best in the world's science and technology and make it the new starting point of our advances";

10. *Time allocation*: The reduction of the amount of time technical personnel spend in political meetings. At least five-sixths of weekly work hours had to be "guaranteed to scientific and technical personnel to engage in professional work";

11. *Budget*: An increase in expenditures from the state budget for science and technology; and,

12. *Publicity*: More publicity for science and technology through special features in newspapers, radio, and television. "Literary and art workers" already had created or were creating works with scientific and educational themes.

Fang's summary and much of the subsequent discussion of the new policy in the Chinese press frequently used such terms as "resuming" and "reestablishing." These terms are significant because they not only signified a break with the policies of the Gang of Four, which were seen as major interruptions of China's scientific development, but also suggested that current policy could be understood by looking at past policy. The relevant past in this instance was the pre–Cultural Revolution period.

This chapter discusses the institutional setting of science and technology by analyzing the national organization of science-related activities and science planning in the context of the shifts in science policy and organization since 1949. The following chapter offers a comparable perspective on those aspects of institutional changes affecting professional life and research administration.

THE ORGANIZATION OF SCIENCE AND TECHNOLOGY

The Science and Technology Commission

The reestablishment of the Science and Technology Commission is the most fundamental reform in the area of policymaking and national administration for science. It is also an important indication that policy thinking derived much more from the pre–Cultural Revolution period than from the Cultural Revolution.

The new commission, according to Fang Yi, was to "take charge of overall planning, coordination, organization and administration of the country's scientific and technological work."[2] Judging from this description, its function resembles that of the pre–Cultural Revolution State Science and Technology Commission (STC), which by the early 1960s was China's leading organ for science planning and administration. The STC was established in 1958 by merging the Science Planning Committee and the State Technological Committee and was responsible to the State Council. The STC, like the Science Planning Committee before it, was a suprasectoral agency that was designed to coordinate the science and technology activities of the Chinese Academy of Sciences and the ministerial and educational sectors. Such coordination was particularly critical after national science planning was introduced in 1956.

The STC exerted widespread influence over the whole range of national science policy questions. It was the key organization in effecting central coordination of the planning processes in each sector, played the major role in preparing and administering the state science budget, and sponsored scientific conferences to generate information for planning purposes. The STC was also active in manpower planning and allocation, in the supply and distribution of scientific instruments, and in the standardization of weights and measures for both research and production. At the provincial and subprovincial levels, the STC delegated authority to and coordinated activities with provincial science and technology committees. The STC also maintained close relations with military research and development. Marshal Nie

Rongzhen was head of both the STC and the separate Science and Technology Commission for National Defense. The senior staff of the STC consisted of nonscientist bureaucrats, who by 1965-66 had become specialists in national science administration.

The original sixteen-point charter of the Cultural Revolution contained instructions that science and technology work should not be disrupted (point 12). As radical interpretations of the social role of science became dominant, however, it was clear that the system of science developed before 1966 was seriously inconsistent with the radical views. Where the radicals stressed the wisdom of the masses as the motive force of scientific development, the science system stressed professional competence. Where the radicals stressed a direct relation between research and production, the system was premised on the structural differentiation of laboratory research and production. The radical view stressed antielitism and egalitarianism; the science and educational systems were clearly elitist and restricted to those who held expert credentials. The radical view was antibureaucratic; the science system was clearly a vast bureaucracy.

It was natural that the Cultural Revolution activists should find those most responsible for creating the science system responsible for these disparities. These included, of course, the leaders of the STC. During the Cultural Revolution, most of these leaders disappeared from public life, and a number of them were subject to public criticism. The commission itself seems to have been disbanded, and many of its functions devolved to the Academy of Sciences and provincial-level authorities.

Efforts to reconstruct the machinery of the central government proceeded spasmodically in the years immediately following the Cultural Revolution and included a fair share of ad hoc administrative arrangements. One such arrangement was the Science and Education Group of the State Council. By 1972, this unit, in conjunction with the CAS, appeared to be performing some of the functions of the old STC.[3] It was headed by Liu Xiyao, a former vice-chairman of the STC, who served as minister of education from 1977 to 1979. Although little is known about the Science and Education Group, it is unlikely that its powers were as extensive as those of its predecessor, the STC. Instead, in the period from 1969 to 1977, centralized policymaking for science and technology, to the extent that it existed, involved cooperative interactions among the Science and Education Group, the Academy of Sciences, the Science and Technology Association, and the State Planning Commission. Although a clearly articulated central structure did not exist, throughout the early 1970s some of the pre–Cultural Revolution science administrators from the STC and elsewhere resumed their former careers either in the Science and Education Group or in one of the other organizations noted above, especially the Secretariat of the Academy of Sciences.

The reestablishment of a Science and Technology Commission can be expected to bring greater coherence and centralization to national science policymaking and to provide a means of mobilizing resources centrally for policy implementation. The commission reportedly has a staff of approximately two hundred, organized in some ten bureaus. The bureaus include one for planning and a number organized according to interdisciplinary mission-oriented principles, including one for energy and petrochemicals and one for computers. In short, the new commission has as its mandate the interpretation, elaboration, and implementation of the new national scientific and technological development plans.

The functions of the STC at the provincial level are performed by science and technology committees closely linked to the office of the secretary of the provincial party committees, as well as to the central STC. Although it appeared that these provincial science and technology committees were strengthened during 1977–78, it was less clear whether provincial jurisdictions continued to control local science-related organizations as extensively as they had since the decentralization measures inspired by the Cultural Revolution were instituted in 1969–70.

By 1979, the role of the communist party in science and technology policy at the highest levels was of great importance, but it was not clear how the central party apparatus was organized to manage science. Before the Cultural Revolution, there were party committees at all levels of the science system, and these were linked to central party organs through an office for science within the party's Propaganda Department. That office was headed in the pre–Cultural Revolution period by Yu Guangyuan, who is now a vice-minister of the STC and a vice-president of the new Academy of Social Sciences. It is possible that the role of the central party apparatus is being de-emphasized in the face of a strong, politically responsible STC headed by an individual who is concurrently a member of the Politburo.

As part of the national effort to strengthen science and technology, party secretaries at the provincial level were instructed to strengthen party leadership in science within their provinces. Reports from a number of provinces throughout the fall of 1977 indicated numerous conferences and other activities designed to familiarize local party officials with the new directions in policy and to gain their active support of them.[4]

In short, many of the policymaking and implementing structures that characterized the highly articulated science policy system of the pre–Cultural Revolution period have been reinstituted. In addition, the leadership positions of these structures have been filled with people of political influence and access to high party circles.

The overall organization of scientific and technological activities is highly variegated and complex. Indeed, it is useful to think of it as a network or system of organizations. The system is differentiated by vertical sectoral distinctions—academic, ministerial, higher educational—and by a horizontal division of centralized versus decentralized administration. In addition, the system is differentiated into organizations responsible for policymaking and administration, for research, for education, and for extension and popularization.

The Chinese Academy of Sciences

The Chinese Academy of Sciences (CAS) has a number of important roles in the new science system. These include shaping policy for basic research, performing both basic and applied research, manufacturing scientific instruments, operating scientific information services, and providing training and educational services.

High-level policy and administrative authority within the CAS before the Cultural Revolution was shared among the officers of the academy (president, vice-presidents), the Secretariat (secretary-general and deputy secretaries-general) and the Party Committee. During the early 1970s, in the absence of a strong STC and given the advanced ages of the president and vice-presidents, the Secretariat probably played the leading role. The appointments of Fang Yi as a vice-president of the academy and of Yu Wen, a seasoned science administrator, as secretary-general can be considered an indication that the academy will continue to play a central role in determining science policy. In particular, the academy can be expected to take the lead in policy and administration for basic research and for advanced training.

The University of Science and Technology, which was established in Beijing as a joint venture in advanced training by the academy and the Ministry of Education in 1958, was reopened after being disrupted by the Cultural Revolution and then moved to Anhui province on the orders of the Gang of Four. Recently it was decided to convert the Heilongjiang Engineering College into the Haerbin University of Science and Technology, administered jointly by the CAS and Heilongjiang province. The primary leadership was to come from the CAS, however, indicating a more active CAS role in higher education. The CAS also has the main leadership role in the Zhejiang University, where CAS Vice-President Qian Sanqiang was made president and in the Chengdu University of Science and Technology. The academy also works closely—by sharing staff and facilities—with other institutions of higher education as well, in order to establish strong programs in the basic sciences. In addition, the CAS has reestablished its own graduate programs and participates in the graduate programs of the University of Science and Technology that are conducted in Beijing.

Policymaking, planning, and coordination within the CAS sector are centered in the academy's Secretariat. Within the Secretariat are five discipline-oriented bureaus—biology; mathematics, physics, and astronomy; new technology (*xin jishu*); chemistry; and earth sciences. These bureaus are for institute leaders points of contact with the central academy administration and important centers for allocative decisions affecting research within the academy sector. Bureau staffs reportedly consist of scientists as well as nonscientists. The academy is in the process of organizing "academic committees" (*xueshu weiyuanhui*) as advisory mechanisms at the bureau level. The academic committees are to include leading scientists within a given discipline both from inside and outside the academy sector. For major projects involving substantial expenditures, the bureaus also convene ad hoc advisory committees of scientists and, where appropriate, engineers and representatives from industry.

The CAS is also the chief performer of advanced basic and much applied research in China. The headquarters of the academy and a number of institutes under its jurisdiction are in Beijing. There are, however, a number of institutes outside Beijing that are also controlled by the CAS. Before the Cultural Revolution, there were approximately 120 institutes under the academy's jurisdiction. One of the main organizational changes resulting from the Cultural Revolution was to reduce that number to 36, and 17 of these were under the joint jurisdiction of the academy and a unit of local government. Most of the other 80–90 institutes were placed under the control of a unit of local government. The trend of policy during the late 1970s has led to the reinstitution of a greater degree of central CAS direction and control. Indeed, by 1979, over one hundred research institutes were under partial CAS control.

What appeared at first sight to have been a trend in the opposite direction was the reestablishment of CAS "branch academies" (*fen yuan*), which were first formed during the Great Leap Forward as part of the decentralization measures of that period. Most of them were abolished in the early 1960s, however. By 1979, new branch academies were established in Shanghai, Sichuan, and Xinjiang, and a number of other provinces. They are viewed as administrative mechanisms in support of decentralization *within* the CAS and are intended to facilitate decision making at the institute, municipal, and provincial levels in order to avoid the need to refer all decisions to Beijing.

During 1977–78, the academy thus seemed to experience a simultaneous centralization with more institutes returned to its control and an internal decentralization with the establishment of the branch academies. The objectives of these moves seemed to be aimed at achieving greater central control and coordination, but at the same time avoiding excessive red tape. However, the fact that CAS jurisdiction over many institutes is still shared with local governments seems to indicate a commitment to keeping the institutes responsive to the needs of their immediate environments.

Institutions of Higher Education

The extent and legitimacy of research in institutes of higher education in China in the past was always unclear. In adopting the Soviet system in the 1950s, the Chinese adopted a system that de-emphasized university research relative to a centralized academy. During the Great Leap Forward period, university research was encouraged, but the emphasis was placed on applied research of direct relevance to problems of production. Since the Cultural Revolution, the research that has been done in universities has tended to follow the style of the Great Leap Forward period.

Under the new policy, university research has been strengthened and expanded into areas of basic and applied research that did not need to be directly relevant to production. As we have seen, there is now a strong concern for quality training in science and technology in order to replace the present generation of senior scientists. At the same time, it is to those senior scientists who are still active that the government has turned for advice for this task. Since most of these men received advanced training at the great universities of the West, where advanced training and research are intimately related, it is plausible to infer that they have recommended more university research. Along with this research there has been curricular reform serving to increase the emphasis on theoretical training compared with recent years. This was what many of these scientists recommended when their views were solicited in 1956, and this was apparently what Zhou Peiyuan recommended in his report of 1972.

In the late seventies, institutions of higher education in China could be divided into the following categories: (1) comprehensive universities, or those offering courses in a broad spectrum of disciplines in the arts and sciences; (2) universities specializing in the sciences or engineering; (3) specialized institutes for particular areas of technology; and (4) workers' universities and schools run by production units. In addition, higher education could also be differentiated by a newly established program for developing centers of excellence. Eighty-eight institutions have been identified for this special attention. In addition, four universities—the University of Science and Technology in Hefei, Anhui province, the Haerbin University of Science and Technology, Zhejiang University, and the Chengdu University of Science and Technology—were operated jointly by the Ministry of Education and the CAS.

All institutions of higher education are under some form of direction from the Ministry of Education, but in addition to the CAS, production ministries (in the case of specialized technical institutes) and local governments also have varying roles in educational administration. Universities receive an annual research budget from the Ministry of Education for research and facilities. As in the CAS sector, research is conducted according to a centrally coordinated plan. The ministry reportedly has an office of science and technology (*keji chu*) responsible for university research at the national level. Many institutions of higher education are also linked to provincial-level education bureaus and provincial science and technology committees. In addition, universities receive projects and funding for applied research from the central Science and Technology Commission and its provincial branches. Finally, university scientists can apply for university-level discretionary funds for projects outside the yearly plans.

Support can come from either the provincial education bureaus or the central Ministry of Education. Generally, funds originating with the central government go directly to the universities from the Ministry of Education. Funds originating at the local level are channeled through the provincial educational bureaus. Such funds typically come from the local science and technology committee, perhaps in response to requests for assistance from local industry or agriculture. At least, some funding for research in specialized technical institutes comes from production ministries. The Ministry of the Petroleum Industry, for instance, has been supplying educational institutions under its purview with the most modern equipment available.

In the past, the universities, generally unlike the CAS, performed contract research. Reportedly university research budgets were not as ample as those of the CAS and were probably kept low to encourage contract work with industry in order to keep research in the educational sector oriented toward "serving the needs of production." With the new emphasis on basic research in the late 1970s and the designation of the universities and the CAS as the chief performers of basic research, central funding through the Ministry of Education and scientist-initiated research activities can be expected to increase.

The Production Ministries

The production ministries of research performers in China comprise the third sector. Within this sector are those ministries having their own academies, such as the Ministry of Agriculture with its recently established commission on agricultural science and technology and its Chinese Academy of Agricultural Sciences and the Ministry of Public Health with its Academy of Medical Sciences and Academy of Traditional Chinese Medicine. Also in this category is the Ministry of Defense, which has its own high-level science policy unit in the National Defense Science and Technology Commission, its own research institutes and Academy of Military Science, its ties with institutes under the CAS, and its own research and production system in the Second to Seventh Ministries of Machine Building. Most other production ministries also have research and training institutions under their jurisdictions.

As in the academy sector, one consequence of the Cultural Revolution was the devolution of control over many research facilities from the central ministries to local governments, or joint center-local direction. The future can be expected to bring greater centralization, but as with the academy, liaison with localities will remain strong.

Research in the ministerial sector was always more oriented toward application compared with research in the academy sector. This difference can be expected to continue. Indeed, one would expect more specialization among the sectors in the future, with the CAS and universities becoming more involved in a strengthened basic research effort and much of the applied work assigned to the ministerial sector.

If our assumptions about the composition of China's pool of scientific manpower are correct and Chinese policy is directed toward the strengthening of a national research and development system to promote science-based technology, then the ministerial sector should become a particularly interesting sector to monitor. It is likely that this sector has the most acute manpower shortage, and new educational policies presumably are directed toward solving that problem. One would expect, therefore, a lag in research and development performance in this sector, pending the education of a new generation of applied scientists and engineers with a strong grounding in basic science.

Greater specialization and differentiation of tasks among the sectors represents a change from the emphasis in post–Cultural Revolution science policy. Because of the peculiar views of scientific development that received institutional support following the Cultural Revolution, policy intentionally attempted to prevent functional differentiation. Thus, institutes in the academy sector as well as the universities organized and supported factories and other production activities, while factories in the ministerial sector established research activities and "universities" (the most famous example is the Shanghai Machine Tools Plant). One of the most important organizational changes implied by the new policy toward science and technology in the late 1970s was the reversal of some of these previous trends. The extent of this reversal and the possible continuation of some of the post-Cultural Revolution experiments—which were intended to link research with production—are interesting questions for the future. One indication of future trends, however, was that the workers' universities, which trained lower-level technical manpower, continued to function in 1979.

The Science and Technology Association

The science system also includes organizations relating to professional life and to popularization and extension. As Fang Yi pointed out in his December 1977 report, the Science and Technology Association was reviving its activities, and professional societies were resuming their work.

The Science and Technology Association (STA) was formed in 1958 to unite professional and popular science by merging the All-China Federation of Scientific Societies and the All-China Society for the Promotion of Scientific and Technical Knowledge. As an organization representing the value of joining the professional with the popular, the STA had a mission that reflected the party's ideologically derived views of science. The STA, however, was not totally immune to sudden shifts in the political winds. The professional societies under the STA's general leadership and direction were disrupted during the Cultural Revolution, and their reestablishment after 1969 was slow and halting. The post–Cultural Revolution role of professional societies, however, had already changed, according to Fang Yi, and they could be expected to become even more active than they were before the Cultural Revolution in sponsoring conferences, supporting publications, conducting international exchanges, and fostering professional development generally.

The STA's work in popularization before the Cultural Revolution was conducted through a decentralized network of local science and technology associations that usually maintained science information centers. The exact fate of these local associations during the Cultural Revolution is unclear, but what is certain is that policy during and after the Cultural Revolution emphasized grass-roots science and technology. This focus on grass-roots science can be expected to continue, and the work of the STA in the area of popularization probably will be strengthened. According to the twelfth point of Fang Yi's speech to the Chinese People's Political Consultation Conference in December 1977, both the mass media and literary and art fields were being mobilized to promote popular understanding of and support for science and technology. The emphasis, however, would probably be more on the popularization of discoveries and innovations of expert scientists and technologists and less on Cultural Revolution themes of the contributions of the masses and the need for the professionals to learn from the masses.

Before the Cultural Revolution, the member societies of the STA were important channels for communicating ideas from the scientific community to science policymakers.[5] According to a 1978 statement by STA chairman Zhou Peiyuan, the societies would again perform this function, and "scientists will have a channel for putting through suggestions for improving education and scientific work and promoting economic growth and defense construction."[6]

China began its push toward the modernization of science and technology with a network of organizations discharging all functions necessary to a science system. Most of these organizations existed before the Cultural Revolution. By the late seventies this network had both national, centralized components and provincial and subprovincial components. It was designed to foster both professional and mass science and innovation and to connect the two. The policies of the Cultural Revolution resulted in greater decentralization of the system; greater emphasis on the mass, rather than the professional components; and the underutilization of the professional components. The new policies introduced in the late 1970s have resulted in a return to the emphasis of the early 1960s and entailed some recentralization and greater attention to professional science and technology. As Fang Yi pointed out, the whole system would also be the beneficiary of greater investments of resources and receive stronger political support than before the Cultural Revolution.

Perhaps the most important observation that can be made about the general organization of the Chinese science system is that much of it was already in place as a result of the organizational innovations of the 1956–66 period. Thus, lack of organization was unlikely to become a major constraint on Chinese scientific development. This is not to say that the system will not encounter organizational problems. However, China did not have to face the costly task, in terms of time and resources, of building a network of organizations de novo. Instead, it needed only to revitalize the moribund network and reactivate some of the dormant components of the system.

PLANNING

One aspect of China's new directions in science and technology that should be of particular interest to students of science policy is the reintroduction of systematic and explicit planning in science and technology. This planning got under way in 1977 and was conducted both centrally in Beijing and at the province level as well, as a result of provincial planning conferences in preparation for the National Science Conference in spring, 1978.

China's planning efforts were conducted under three time horizons, with 1977 as the base year. The first was a three-year plan to 1980, the second the eight-year plan discussed in the preceding chapter, and the third a 23-year plan to the year 2000. The three-year plan appeared to be a compensatory program for overcoming some of the weaknesses in the system resulting from the discredited policies of the post–Cultural Revolution period. A major priority during this period was to reform the educational system so that manpower constraints could be overcome quickly. Hence, considerable effort was expended after 1977 to expand enrollments in higher education, initiate graduate programs in the CAS and institutions of higher education, and organize training programs in foreign countries.[7] At the secondary education level, the plan called for making middle school education universal in the cities and junior middle school universal in the countryside by 1985.[8]

Additional objectives included the establishment of a number of new research centers and large new laboratories and the strengthening of such auxiliary and support activities as scientific information services, the production of scientific instruments, and the rationalization of standards needed for major research and development efforts during the remainder of this century. As part of this logistical effort, attempts to rationalize administrative procedures, including planning procedures themselves, were to be made.

The plan for 1985 assumes that the goals of the three-year plan have been achieved. By 1985, the Chinese hope to have a finely tuned, effective, and comprehensive research and development system in operation. In addition, the plan calls for the achievement of world levels in certain selected fields of science by 1985. The goal of the 23-year plan is to elevate most areas of Chinese science and technology to world levels.

Chinese discussions of these planning efforts frequently mention the tonic effects on scientific development resulting from the earlier twelve-year plan that began in 1956 and of the ten-year plan of 1962. The twelve-year plan (1956–67) took well over a year to prepare and was chiefly the responsibility of the Academy of Sciences and the predecessor of the STC, the Science Planning Committee. Although some of China's scientists opposed the introduction of planning at the time, in retrospect the twelve-year plan appears to have contributed to China's scientific development in several ways. First, it helped to clarify priorities among a number of different areas of research. Although over 500 projects were included in the plan, twelve areas were singled out for special attention.[9] As priorities were set, the planning process also led to the establishment of fields of science that were weak or nonexistent in China. Second, the comprehensive plan also indicated the financial and human resources, equipment, facilities, and technical services needed to meet objectives at different stages of the plan's implementation. It also identified areas where foreign assistance from the Soviet bloc countries was required, and indeed in its final form, the plan was reviewed by the Soviet Union. Third, planning for science and technology was synchronized with economic planning and development. Included here were considerations of regional development and the geographical distribution of economic, scientific, and technological activities. Finally, the preparation of the twelve-year plan involved the active participation of scientists in the planning process, and since the CAS had the central role, it entailed certain structural changes in the academy.[10]

The planning activities that began in 1977 seemed to have many of the same objectives. The new plans are cumulative, comprehensive, and closely linked with economic and military objectives. An outline plan for basic science was developed at a conference in Beijing in October 1977 attended by some 1,200 scientists and administrators. It called for active efforts by the CAS and universities to establish a well-developed "research network" in basic science by 1985. This was integrated with plans of the Science and Technology Commission for applied research, manpower development, and other fields of scientific activity. If past practices are followed, this process of aggregation and refinement will be supplemented by ad hoc conferences and consultations with professional societies in order to open the planning process to both vertical sectoral interests and horizontal, intersectoral interests.

The twelve-year plan was supplemented by annual plans, and planning became a matter of routine by the early 1960s, particularly after the establishment of the STC. Reportedly many of the objectives of the twelve-year plan were achieved ahead of schedule, and as a result, a new ten-year plan was drawn up in 1962–63. This plan and the planning system for science and technology were extensively disrupted by the Cultural Revolution. No serious planning efforts were undertaken after the Cultural Revolution until the ouster of the Gang of Four.

The pre–Cultural Revolution planning system was, on the whole, favorable to the development of Chinese science. It did, however, extend state control over science. From the point of view of the individual scientist, the inclusion of his or her area of research within the plan was the difference between being able to continue a line of inquiry or not. The great virtue of the reintroduction of planning in the late seventies for both scientists and administrators was that it introduced an important element of stability and predictability into professional life which had not been present since the beginning of the Cultural Revolution. Thus, the reintroduction of extensive national planning, coupled as it was with generous and influential political support, was probably received enthusiastically by most of China's scientists.

However, planning for the last quarter of the twentieth century can be expected to differ in important ways from the preparations surrounding the twelve-year plan in the 1950s. In the earlier period, one of the objectives was to identify certain key fields of science that were totally absent in China and to make provisions for their development. The objective of the policy was known. By the 1970s, most fields of science were represented in China. The task became one of anticipating internal developments within fields and phasing with them in order to reach a stage of parity with advanced world levels in some fields by 1985 and in all fields by the year 2000.

Similarly, synchronization of scientific and economic plans in the earlier period involved fairly basic and, in some cases, primitive levels of technology. In the earlier period, China's basic industrial structure was still being organized. The operative question for the science planner then was: What will be the research and development needs of, for instance, an infant electronics industry? Or, if a petrochemical plant is to be built in location X, what will be the needed science and technology facilities for its support?

Although China's industrial structure in the late 1970s was clearly still evolving, much more of it was in place than was the case in the 1950s and early 1960s, and the levels of technology were markedly higher. The issue confronting planners was the probable trends within a given area of industrial or agricultural technology, rather than the establishment of a given area of technology. The contrast was between planning for a reasonably well known objective and planning for what were in principle unknowable future conditions.

The processes and assumptions used in Chinese science planning are not known outside of China. However, it is plausible to suggest that science planning in China for the remainder of this century will be a far more sophisticated task than was the preparation of the twelve-year plan. The informational and analytical requirements are quite different, and there are indications that the Chinese realize this. There have been suggestions, for instance, that there will be a need for what we in the West might call scientific and technological forecasting. In the late 1970s it was unclear who in China was prepared to meet the informational and analytical needs of science planning, although there was evidence of such preparations beginning at the Academy of Social Sciences and elsewhere. The values contained in the new policy, especially the value of expertise, suggested that China was preparing to encourage the development of new professional roles specifically committed to science planning and the social studies of science.[11] Such an innovation was also consistent with the strengthening of the social and behavioral sciences, fields long neglected in China, but in the late seventies enjoying a degree of legitimacy that they had not had for many years.

In addition to the analytic problems of planning for the 1980s and 1990s, the question of plan implementation raises some potential administrative problems that could be more severe than those of the past. The establishment of comprehensive planning offers the prospect, in principle, of matching research and development with the technical needs of production and defense. The achievement of these matches will require organizational linkages, and these linkages will be essential for the research-driven innovation China expects from its investment in research and development. Such linkages are problematic in both capitalist and socialist economies. Whether China can maintain the linkages in an environment of rapidly expanding expenditures and capital construction remains to be seen. This subject is explored further at the end of the following chapter.

The discussion thus far has been concerned with the macro-organization of the Chinese science system and how the new policy will affect that organization. There are, however, two other questions that relate to the institutional setting of Chinese science. These are what might be called "micro-organizational" questions concerning professional life, and research administration at the institute and laboratory levels. These are the subjects of chapter 3.

Chapter Three

◆ ◆ ◆

Professional Life and Research Administration

It is not an overstatement to say that the very existence of professional life among China's scientists has been an issue in science policy debates over the years. My use of the term "professional" is intended to convey the idea that certain groups in society possessing certain critical skills are differentiated from the rest of society on the basis of those skills. For those possessing skills and expertise, a measure of social autonomy is required if the full exercise of expertise is to be realized. In turn, the professional group exists in a fiduciary relationship with society, one aspect of which is the internal governance and maintenance of quality within the profession.

At a fairly early stage, the Chinese Communist Party rejected this Western interpretation of professionalism. In particular, the party rejected the idea of autonomous, self-governing groups in society and insisted that since science is to serve society, and is to be supported by societal resources, then society should exercise control over science. Much of the politics of science in the mid-1950s involved reconciling scientists to this idea of societal control exercised through the party and the state. This reconciliation finally entailed a compromise between purely professional and purely state or bureaucratic values. Under the compromise, full professional autonomy was sacrificed to a measure of bureaucratic and political control and accountability, but in return the state tacitly recognized that scientific work is not analogous to factory production. Hence, special regard had to be given to the professional requirements of scientists, their work environments, uses of time, goals, and incentives. This bureaucratic-professional compromise was not unlike patterns of accommodation found in both the Soviet Union and in nonuniversity research settings in the United States.[1]

There was, however, another faction within the party that saw in this compromise a threat to the development and egalitarian goals of the revolution. Adherents of this view saw in the compromise a capitulation to elitism and a commitment to a pattern of scientific development inimical to the interests of the broad masses of the population. This strongly antiprofessional or, more accurately, anti–bureaucratic-professional view of science was influential during the Great Leap Forward and became the dominant view during and immediately after the Cultural Revolution. From the point of view of the individual Chinese scientist, the greatest change entailed by the new science policy of 1977–78 was that this radical view of science was rejected and the bureaucratic-professional compromise—with its recognition of the value of expertise and of the requirements for the exercise of expertise—was reinstituted. Under the new policies, however, professional norms and values were legitimated to an extent not seen since the mid-1950s.

The strong antiprofessional or anti–bureaucratic-professional view originated in certain strands of modern Chinese history related to the issues of elitism, foreign culture, and the tolerance of heterodox ideas. For the citizen of Western industrialized democracies, there is increasing concern over the accountability and responsibility of scientific and technocratic elites. While such concern has been and will continue to be real and well founded, there is also, in China, a special concern about elitism, which derives from twentieth-century reactions to Confucianism. Confucian China, one should recall, was an elitist society in which power and prestige were reserved for those who had mastered the learned tradition. The particular relation between learning and social position which was Confucianism forms the basis of the link between anti-intellectualism and antielitism in modern China. As interest in modern science began to develop in China and particularly as the spirit, procedures, and values of science, as opposed to its mere pragmatic value, became appreciated, science became for some a surrogate ideology for Confucianism.[2] Although those holding this ideology were never serious contenders for political power and although the actual behavior of many Chinese scientists prior to 1949 was a far cry from that of the Confucian literati, the identification of those possessing socially valued knowledge with elitism has remained strong and politically salient. To the extent that professionalism entails special status (as it does by definition), one of the roots of antiprofessionalism in Communist China can be identified.

Antielitism, however, is but one aspect of antiprofessionalism. Another is the historic uneasiness with foreign learning and culture characteristic of both the Confucian traditionalist and the anti-Confucian revolutionary. For the former, foreign learning threatened to invalidate Confucian learning and hence the Confucian social order. Twentieth-century Chinese revolutionaries on the other hand were, in rejecting Confucianism, rejecting both an old order for its own sake and an old order that, in its weakness, allowed Chinese sovereignty to be compromised by imperialist powers. The Chinese revolution, of course, has had strong nationalistic themes, and these have extended to issues of culture and learning. Twentieth-century proponents of modern science have always run the risk of being classified as "worshippers of things foreign" and of being inappropriately cosmopolitan and hence out of phase with Chinese nationalism.

Although nationalism in science and technology in the People's Republic has had many beneficial effects—for instance, in calling attention to relevant knowledge in traditional medicine, seismology, climatology, and agriculture—it has been problematic for the development of professionalism in science. To the extent that professionalism involves cosmopolitanism, a second source of antiprofessionalism can be found in the profound skepticism of cosmopolitanism that is reflected in the Chinese revolution.[3]

A final factor contributing to antiprofessionalism is the low tolerance shown by regimes with totalitarian ideologies for heterodox ideas and cultural pluralism. In this sense there has unfortunately been a basic continuity between Confucianism and Chinese communism. Professionalism implies the existence of certain bodies of socially useful and intrinsically interesting knowledge that cannot be subsumed logically under a dominant political ideology. Therefore, the organization and governance of those with direct access to that knowledge must be excepted from the organization and governance within the dominant ideology. Although toleration of heterodoxy has been a problem for other communist nations as well, the Confucian tradition may have made this a particularly difficult problem for the Chinese to solve.

These three sources of antiprofessionalism have combined to make professional life a core issue for party policy toward intellectuals. Formal policy toward intellectuals has remained fairly constant over the years. The actual treatment of intellectuals, however, has varied significantly from period to period, and scientists, because of their potential contributions to economic and military development, have been treated differently and more preferentially than other intellectuals. Since the start of the Cultural Revolution, however, the treatment of nearly all intellectuals has been consistently bad.

The problem for the party has been that the intellectuals from the old society were mainly from nonrevolutionary classes. Although many of them showed sympathy for the revolution and although their talents were needed for Chinese development, their class backgrounds and, for many, their foreign training always created doubts about their political reliability.

China's long-term goal has been to replace these "bourgeois intellectuals" with "proletarian intellectuals," but over the short term, a policy for handling the former was needed. This policy has been for the party, and the proletariat generally, to unite with the intellectuals and transform them through ideological remolding. The great majority of intellectuals were seen as friendly to the revolution and loyal to the regime. Ideological remolding through political meetings and, at times, through physical labor was intended to overcome the influence of bourgeois backgrounds.

In addition, organizational control was extended over intellectuals as well. In science, the Party built on the organizational resources of the professional societies to form the All-China Federation of Scientific Societies, which in 1958 became part of the Science and Technology Association. Although professional societies were instruments of political control, prior to the Cultural Revolution they were also active in genuine scientific activities. The Cultural Revolution disrupted these societies and called into question their legitimacy. The questions raised concerned not only the legitimacy of professionalism, but also the political rectitude of nonscientist science administrators who accommodated demands for a differentiated if not autonomous professional life.

Well after the Cultural Revolution, these themes were maintained by the Gang of Four and their followers. After late 1976, however, the Gang of Four's position was criticized as a fundamentally mistaken interpretation of the policy toward intellectuals. Instead of recognizing the loyalty and contributions of intellectuals and the progress made in uniting with and transforming them, the Gang of Four allegedly saw the older intellectuals as class enemies. The gang was particularly critical of the educational system that was to produce the proletarian intellectuals required for the long-term solution of the intellectuals problem. This critique was contained in the now widely publicized and widely denounced Gang of Four doctrine of the "two estimates," according to which (1) during the seventeen years between 1949 and 1966, the educational policies of Chairman Mao were by and large not carried out, leading to a situation in education in which the bourgeoisie "exercised dictatorship" over the proletariat and not vice versa; and, as a result, (2) the students trained in those years were basically bourgeois in their world outlook. Hence they were bourgeois, not proletarian intellectuals, who belonged to the "stinking ninth category" of class enemies.[4]

The changes brought about as a result of the purge of the Gang of Four repudiated this interpretation of intellectuals and their role in society. Indeed, in the late seventies intellectuals were being praised and honored in ways that had not been seen in over twenty years.

The impact of this change on professional life can be appreciated by examining some of the components of that life. The first involves the recruitment into professional roles and professional socialization. Recruitment and socialization, as the Gang of Four realized, were intimately related to the education system, its content, and the criteria used for admission. The reforms following the Cultural Revolution emphasized extrascientific criteria in determining admission to higher education. Questions of political achievement and work performance figured prominently and at times outweighed aptitude and academic achievement. Similarly, once students were recruited, the official socialization stressed extrascientific values of service to the people and the importance of correct political understanding.

It appears that the new policy is intended to change these recruitment and socialization practices. It is now no longer necessary for the aspiring scientist or technologist to complete a work assignment prior to enrollment and be recommended for higher education by those in his workplace. Academic criteria clearly replaced political considerations as the principal determinants of admission to higher education.

During the first year of the new policy, 30 percent of the new university class were to be enrolled directly from senior-middle-school graduates without the interruption of a mandatory stint of physical labor. As we have seen, entrance examinations were reintroduced.[5] Recognition of the value of expertise should mean that the content of the socialization will be much less concerned with values extrinsic to science, although the emphasis on public service and correct politics will not be abandoned completely.

One of the professional values sacrificed in the bureaucratic-professional compromise mentioned earlier was that of individual determination of job mobility. Scientists and engineers were assigned employment by political authorities. Under the bureaucratic-professional compromise, however, these assignments were made with due regard to the competencies involved as well as to the organizational needs of the state. In the post–Cultural Revolution period, however, these latter two considerations were apparently seriously and widely ignored. A serious mismatching of jobs and skills and an underemployment of technical manpower resulted. Much of this could be attributed to policies intended to familiarize technical personnel with the concrete problems of the Chinese masses and to contribute to their ideological remolding.

Although efforts to expose scientists and technologists to grass-roots problems are likely to continue, the new leaders felt that the mismatching of skills to tasks had to be rectified. Hence, the fifth point of Fang Yi's twelve-point program called attention to "extensive investigations" of cases where technical personnel "cannot apply at their present posts what they have learned at school," with the intent of making necessary readjustments.[6]

Discussions of the new policy throughout 1977 suggested that this underutilization was widespread. Authorities at all levels were instructed by Beijing to remedy this situation, and reports of provincial meetings called to implement the new science policy frequently mentioned the reassignment of technical personnel as an important initial task. Hence, although the principle of job assignment by political authorities has not been abandoned, the new policy is strongly committed to employing people in positions where their expertise is both needed and appreciated.

Despite the intent of the new policy, however, there have been indications that the policy has been resisted both by local-level cadres who continue to exercise "dictatorship" over intellectuals "sent down" to do manual labor and by the intellectuals themselves. The latter reportedly have been reluctant to reassume positions of higher status and responsibility because of fears of yet another policy change that would expose them to the physical and psychological abuses of mass criticism. It is difficult to determine how widespread this phenomenon of resistance has been, but its existence clearly could prolong the underutilization of technical manpower.[7]

A third area of professional life concerns rewards and incentives. In the pre–Cultural Revolution period, a fairly elaborate system of rewards and incentives involving pay scales, ranks and titles, and awards and prizes was established, although efforts were made to downplay such purely professional rewards as colleague recognition. The Cultural Revolution obliterated most of this system and substituted nothing in its place except a rather diffuse acknowledgement of gratitude for service to the people. In particular, ranks and titles and awards and prizes were abolished, and pay scales were frozen into an inequitable pattern in which senior scientists continued to receive among the highest salaries in the country and junior scientists received little more than experienced workers.

The new policy can be expected to change this situation. There has already been some indication that material incentives are to again be used throughout the economy, and the education and work of younger scientists, as well as of senior men, will be recognized with salaries near the top of the national scale. Ranks within the Academy of Sciences have been reestablished, and long delayed promotions have been made, reportedly to the acclaim of all. Prizes and awards have been reinstituted to recognize outstanding effort and achievement, and a new law providing for rewards for inventions and innovations has been promulgated (see Appendix 2).

Professional communication in written form through the scientific literature and in oral form at conferences and professional meetings is central to science. Such communication normally transcends national boundaries, but the pattern of professional communications within a country is a good indicator of the nature of the national scientific community as well.

In the late seventies, China's new science policy seemed to be committed to the support of professional communication to an extent that had not been seen since the early 1960s when professional meetings were held frequently and an indigenous, archival journal literature was developing. The antiprofessional themes of the Cultural Revolution and post–Cultural Revolution periods worked against intraelite scientific communication in the name of elite-mass communication and integration. Few professional meetings were held and those meetings concerned with science and technology that were held were normally more for the social purposes of integrating scientists with the masses than for purposes of scientific communication as that term is usually understood. Similarly, the indigenous journal literature that was developing in the early 1960s was discontinued, and even by 1977, the status of the professional literature had not risen to the pre-1966 level.

Reports since the latter half of 1977 indicated that serious attention was being given to professional communications. Of particular interest were the convening of seminars and small conferences on selected fields of science. In late summer, 1977, for instance, meetings were held on elementary particles and on atrsophysics at scenic Huangshan in Anhui province. The latter meeting was attended by some 120 people, who heard approximately 100 papers. It was the largest such gathering ever held in China and was also used to plan future research.[8]

The meeting on elementary particles was attended by about 130 people of different age groups from research institutes and universities. More than forty papers were presented, including one by Nobel laureate C. N. Yang of the State University of New York at Stony Brook. In addition to the particular interest engendered by Yang's presence, this meeting was noteworthy for the questions it raised about the philosophical and methodological problems surrounding elementary particle physics and for the fuller cooperation it encouraged between scientists and philosophers.[9] It is interesting that both meetings involved fields of science where most work is basic research.

Closely related to scholarly communications is the status of professional organizations. Chief among these is the STA, formed in 1958 as a "peak organization" of China's discipline-oriented and science-popularization societies. Although the STA was not disbanded during the Cultural Revolution, most of its member societies ceased operations, including the convening of professional meetings and the publication of specialized journals.

The status of professional societies and of their communications services was somewhat ambiguous between 1969 and 1976. From time to time, there were indications that these central features of professional life would be strengthened, but the antiprofessional influence of the party's radical elements apparently prevented this. The ambiguity now, however, has been removed, and the new policy clearly calls for the buttressing of the activities of professional organizations and the expansion of communications activities.[10] Following the pattern of the early 1960s, meetings sponsored by professional societies can be expected both to perform the purely professional function of information exchange and to provide information for policymakers and planners.

In early 1979, the extent and character of China's participation in the communications networks of international science remained to be seen. The nearly autarchic avoidance of international communications that characterized certain periods since the start of the Cultural Revolution had certainly given way to greater involvement. But even in China's most internationalist periods, the international relations of Chinese science have always been strictly subordinate to political considerations that dampened the full development of international professional ties. One could argue that fairly tight and narrowly conceived political control will continue. The more likely case was that China's political leaders perceived conditions in the late 1970s and expected conditions in the 1980s to be so different that they concluded that it was in the national interest to develop international communications and encourage cooperation in ways never allowed before. This question is explored more fully in chapters 5 and 6.

Professional life in China is affected by two other factors that are not normally of special interest in other countries. The first concerns what may be called extraprofessional political responsibilities. Since the early 1950s, China's scientists have been expected to participate in political life, primarily through discussion groups and groups devoted to ideological remolding. Such activities will undoubtedly continue. However, over the years, the actual importance attached to such political participation, as measured for instance in the amount of time per week devoted to it, has varied and has been the subject of some debate. During the Great Leap Forward years, the amount of time increased dramatically, as it did in the Cultural Revolution. In the early 1960s, in response to the excesses of the Great Leap Forward, the authorities instituted the five-sixths rule, under which professional personnel were assured that five-sixths of their time could be devoted to professional activities free from political meetings. The new policies of 1977–78 reaffirmed this right.[11]

The other, somewhat unique aspect of professional life in China is the relation among different scientific generations. These intergenerational relations have three dimensions. One is simply the difference in chronological ages. The second concerns differences among age groups based on the different scientific traditions dominant during the professional socialization of the scientists in each group, such as the Western "bourgeois" tradition, the Soviet tradition, and the post-Liberation indigenous tradition. Finally, there are superior-subordinate differences based on formal position in the organization in which a scientist works, a relationship that has been a function of age and training.

These generational factors possess a unique importance in China because of the long Confucian tradition of honoring elders and respecting hierarchy and because of a certain adulation shown by some twentieth-century Chinese intellectuals toward foreign learning and those who have studied abroad. There has long been a strong antipathy in Chinese communism for all three of these conditions. As a result, science policy during more radical periods, such as the Great Leap Forward and the Cultural Revolution, tended to encourage intergenerational conflict in the name of opposing the persistence of Confucian remnants and blind worship of things foreign.

The new policy was announced with a celebration of the achievements and public service attitudes of the senior scientists. From the radical point of view, this celebration was probably construed as an intentional or inadvertent justification of the persistence of the three conditions noted above. It seems, however, that the intention of the new policy is to render generational considerations irrelevant by emphasizing, recognizing, and rewarding achievement rather than age, background, and position.

RESEARCH ADMINISTRATION

One area of scientific and technological activity that will be much affected by the new directions in Chinese policy is the administration of research and development at the working level. This area is related to questions of national planning and organization and to issues of professional life. However, research administration at the microlevel is analytically distinct from issues of professionalism discussed above. It has over the years been an issue of policy and of the politics of science. For these reasons, it warrants separate treatment.

In the pre–Cultural Revolution period, the organization and administration of research institutes gradually evolved toward a system in which the institutes were usually led by competent, experienced scientists holding the position of director. Institutes usually had one or more deputy directors, at least one of whom was a nonscientist with political and administrative responsibilities. The director and deputy directors were assisted in their work by two main committees composed of the institute's members. One committee dealt with academic affairs and the other with administrative affairs. In addition, each institute had a party committee.

This system of structurally differentiating academic, administrative, and political matters was challenged somewhat during the Great Leap Forward, but it reemerged and was strengthened in the early 1960s. During the Cultural Revolution, the administration of research institutes was attacked. A new form of administrative organization, the "revolutionary committee," fused the functions of academic planning, general administration, and political work. Although in many cases individuals who held leadership roles under the old system continued to hold leadership positions, the revolutionary committees were to be more "democratic" by including workers, lower-ranking technicians, and younger scientists. The revolutionary committees were supposed to embody the "three-in-one" combination, which was either interpreted to mean younger, middle-aged, and senior scientists on the one hand, or to mean scientists, state and party cadres, and technicians and workers on the other.

The structure and representation of leadership groups in institutes are important because they reflect the decisional criteria that are to be applied in the selection, control, and evaluation of projects. In the pre-1966 system, leading scientists and nonscientist administrators, as we have seen, reached an accommodation between professional interests and values and state demands and bureaucratic routines. Thus, scientists accepted the reality of national- and institute-level plans, the need for accountability, and the inclusion of nonscientific criteria in decision making. Administrators, in turn, welcomed the inclusion of professional judgments in the planning process and were being sensitized to the qualitative difference between the administration of research and production.

During the Cultural Revolution (and to some extent the Great Leap Forward), the assumptions and values of the bureaucratic-professional accommodation, including both the legitimacy and importance of state plans and the value of professional judgments, were challenged and attacked. Instead, the tenets of party ideology—that research should serve production and that problems for research should come from production practice—were interpreted rather literally. As a result, the criteria for project selection and evaluation were considered best realized when administrative structures in institutes represented the interests of the masses and the institutional boundaries between research institutes and production settings were eliminated through a policy of "open door" research that sent researchers out to factories and brought workers into institutes.

China's new policy has been directed toward reversing these Cultural Revolution trends and returning to administrative structures and procedures similar to those of the early 1960s. Indeed, the second point of Fang Yi's twelve-point program stated that the party's Central Committee had approved a system in which directors of scientific research institutions assumed responsibility under the guidance of party committees.[12]

The one difference from the earlier period is that the commitment of political leaders to the values of professionalism is stronger than it was before the Cultural Revolution. The modernization of science and technology has been made an unambiguous priority. Nonscientist administrators and party cadres involved with research and development have been enjoined to respect the views of and render all possible assistance to the scientist-leaders of research institutes.

The significance of these changes can be appreciated by studying the structure of research administration more closely. The CAS is used as an example below, but the basic principles involved—the juxtaposition of administrative staff activities and professional advisory committees—applies to other sectors as well.

Under the new policy a typical CAS institute is led by a director, usually a scientist, and three or four deputy directors, some of whom are scientists. For research purposes institutes are subdivided into laboratories (typically from five to ten), which in turn are divided into research groups and teams. During a visit to China in May and June 1978, I was told that for research planning and administration, an institute was to have one office for equipment and logistical support and one for research administration. These offices are usually led and staffed by people with some scientific training. The activities of the research administration office are of particular interest. This office is responsible for developing research plans for the institute, for administering the plans, for coordinating with other institutes and organizations, and for providing training for research personnel. Working with the laboratories, it develops planning recommendations. These recommendations are then passed on to the newly reestablished institute-level academic committee for deliberation. Institute academic committees are composed of 20–30 leading scientists and high administrators. In addition to their role in planning, they also review and evaluate the research work done in the institute.

Much of the policy and program initiative seems to originate with the research administration office. Nevertheless, the existence of the academic committee and the opportunity it has to review the work of the research administration office insures that the interests of the working professional scientist are heard. If conflicts develop between this office and the academic committee, they are referred to the director and the party committee for resolution.

Policy statements in the late seventies clearly reaffirmed the ultimate authority of the party to make decisions. For almost thirty years, party policy has been that scientific development in China must proceed under the leadership of the party. The idea of party leadership in science has often been problematic, however. Party cadres usually were not trained in science and therefore had to rely on scientists to clarify complex issues. In addition, party cadres quite often were culturally distant from scientists. Typically the latter were the most highly educated and cosmopolitan group in Chinese society; the former were often of peasant background, without a great deal of formal education. Moreover, cadres were strongly committed to the values of populism and nationalism which blend with Marxism-Leninism in Chinese ideology. Consequently cadres encountered difficulties observing the correct line in research administration. On one hand, they risked relinquishing their leadership role in the face of the complexities of modern science. On the other, they risked exercising authority in an ignorant, boorish, and oppressive way. Part of the cadres' problem was to understand in their own ideological terms the nature of scientific research and the class affiliation of scientists.

As differences over science policy became acute in the early 1970s, the issues of party leadership in research administration, professionalism, and the ideological status of science began to converge. The discussion proceeded in terms of the latter, specifically over the question of whether science was part of the superstructure or, as a "productive force," part of the economic base. In Marxism, the superstructure is a reflection of the economic base, which includes the productive forces.

The Gang of Four considered science, like culture, part of the super-structure. Since the superstructure theoretically reflects the interests of those who control the economic base, science, to the Gang of Four, had to become proletarian science. But, as we have seen, according to the two estimates, science and education were still controlled by the bourgeoisie. Science, as represented by China's professional scientists, was considered a remnant of the superstructure of a bourgeois society. Party leadership in science there-fore entailed exercising proletarian dictatorship over science, and the relation between the cadre and the scientist was considered antagonistic.

It is against this background that the new directions in policy must be analyzed. One of the most important statements in support of the new policy was Deng Xiaoping's speech to the National Science Conference on March 18, 1978.[13] This policy statement envisioned important changes in the role of the party in research administration. The speech, however, did not begin with a discussion of research administration. Instead, it started with a discussion of what, for the occasion, would seem to have been a rather arcane matter, the superstructure/productive forces issue. Deng's position was that science is in fact a productive force, not part of the superstructure, and Deng attempted to document this position with references to Marx and to historical experience. Of the latter, Deng wrote:

> Modern science has opened the way for the progress of production techniques and determined the direction of their development. Many new instruments of production and technological processes have come into being first in the laboratory. A series of newborn industries, including high polymer synthesis, atomic energy, electronic computers, semiconductors, astronautics and laser, have been founded on the basis of newly emerged science and technology.

Deng then went on to link this conception of science to the proper way of viewing scientists. The recognition that

> science and technology are productive forces brings the following question in its train: How should we regard the mental labor involved in scientific pursuits? Since science is becoming an increasingly important part of the production

forces, are people engaged in scientific and technological work to be considered workers or not?

With a few minor qualifications, Deng's answer was that in a socialist society scientists are workers. The main difference "between them and the manual workers lies only in a different role in the social division of labor."

After discussing in general terms the need to expand China's pool of red-and-expert scientists and technologists, Deng focused on the question of party leadership in science. He referred to Hua Guofeng's analysis that China had entered a new stage in which the achievement of the four modernizations is the dominant political task: "To meet the requirements of the new situation and the new task, there must be corresponding changes in the center of gravity for Party work and in the Party's work style." Deng then went on to say that

> professional scientists and technicians form the mainstay of the revolutionary movement for scientific experiment. Without a strong contingent of professional scientific researchers of high caliber, we could hardly scale the heights of modern science and technology, and it would be difficult for the scientific experiment movement of the masses to advance wave upon wave in a sustained way.

From these remarks by Deng, we can infer that party leadership in the administration of research was viewed as a task of critical national importance. But the approach China took to this question in the late 1970s differed radically from anything China had seen since 1966, as the following excerpt shows:

> We should give the director and the deputy directors of research institutes a free hand in the work of science and technology according to their division of labour. Party committees should back up the work of all Party and non-Party experts in administrative positions and try to bring out all their capacities so that they really have powers and responsibilities commensurate with their positions. These experts are also cadres of the Party and the state. We must never look askance at them. Party committees should get acquainted with their work and examine it but should not attempt to supplant them.

Deng emphasized the role of the party as a facilitator of research whose job is to insure that facilities, supplies, supporting services, and general working conditions are adequate for the task. As Deng himself put it to the scientists at the conference, "I am willing to be the director of the logistics department at your service."

To drive home to the party its proper new role, Deng stated that the basic task of research institutes

> is to produce scientific results and train competent people. They must show more scientific and technical achievements of high quality and train scientific

and technical personnel who are both red and expert. *The main criterion for judging the work of the Party committee of a scientific research institute should be the successful fulfillment of this basic task. Only when this is well done has the Party committee really done its duty to consolidate the dictatorship of the proletariat and build socialism.* Otherwise, putting politics in command will remain mere empty talk. (Emphasis added.)

The redefinition of science as a productive force, the reinterpretation of the status of scientists, and the identification of the work of professional scientists with the key political tasks of achieving the four modernizations were all consistent with the redefinition of party leadership. Deng's treatment of these questions clearly indicated that in exerting their authority at the institute level, party committees must incorporate into their decisions the values, perspectives, and interests of professional scientists. Thus, the reestablishment of academic committees in research institutes was important not only because it formally incorporated representatives of scientists into the decision-making process, but also because the political environment was being prepared to be especially receptive to the views of these representatives.

INSTITUTIONAL CONSTRAINTS

In the last two chapters, I have suggested that China was fortunate in having a reasonably well developed network of science- and technology-related institutions on which to build. This network consisted of institutions ranging from those capable of doing sophisticated basic research at one extreme to those doing agricultural and industrial extension at the other. This is not to say, however, that China's ambitious goals for science and technology will not encounter institutional problems. Indeed, policy statements made in 1978 indicated that additional attention was to be given to strengthening that network. An attempt is made below to identify a few of the more serious problems, some of which have their analogues in other nations.

The first of these potential problems concerns basic research. Chinese leaders have indicated that they hope to encourage and expand support for basic research because of their belief in its long-term importance for applications. However, an informal rule sometimes used by students of research and development is that lacking special, countervailing, institutional arrangements, applied research always drives out basic research. At present, it is difficult to see what those special, countervailing institutional arrangements might be in China. The mere assignment of basic research tasks to the CAS and to universities is probably not enough. True basic research may require administrative structures characterized by considerably more autonomy than Chinese society has tolerated in the past.

The second question concerns China's ability to sustain high levels of political support and funding over a significant period of time. As many who have reviewed the goals of the four modernizations have observed, China's plate is very full, and it appears to want to accomplish many resource-consuming goals all at once.

The remarkable support Chinese science has come to enjoy is premised on the contributions expected of it. It is not clear whether science and technology can satisfy all these expectations. If they fail, one wonders what or who will sustain the support, especially since sustaining such support requires communication and understanding between political leaders and the technical community. Such communication and understanding seem to have developed. But political and scientific leaders will inevitably change. Enduring institutionalized means for maintaining political support for science and technology had not developed by 1979, even though the incumbent head of the STC, Fang Yi, was concurrently a member of the Politburo and the whole party was formally mobilized to support scientific development.

The third possible area of institutional failure concerns administrative capabilities, which is foremost an issue of general administrative flexibility in a highly bureaucratized society like China. Flexibility is required for creative administrative responses to imaginative initiatives from scientists and engineers. Flexibility is also required to avoid sectionalism that would threaten communication and cooperation within and among the different sectors of the science system.

The question of administrative capabilities also pertains to the planning process. Planning can play an important role in China's ability to reach its objectives. Priorities do have to be set, resources do have to be mobilized, and difficult decisions do have to be made. This planning question extends to imported technology as well, as chapter 5 points out. The planning tasks require both the analytic skills necessary to maintain some sort of synoptic view of science and technology activities and a sense of strategy to insure that the de facto priorities result from something more than the compromises and incremental adjustments made in response to forces exerted in the political process. The mechanism for accomplishing these planning tasks presumably exists in the STC. It remains to be seen how well it will perform them.

A related institutional question of great importance concerns technological innovation. "Technological innovation is more than R & D,"[14] and if research and development are to fulfill their promise, the rest of the innovation chain must be in place. There must be effective organizational linkages not only between research and production, but also between production and end users.[15]

Some would argue that in socialist economies the innovation chain is particularly hard to maintain. Berliner's studies of the Soviet economy indicated problems with price structures that undervalue new products, decision rules that lead to conservative choices, and a system of incentives that does not reward risk taking.[16]

Interestingly, Fang Yi alluded to this problem of innovation in his speech to the National Science Conference. In a section of his report entitled "Speed Up Popularization and Application of Scientific and Technical Achievements and New Technologies," Fang stated:

> It is a growing trend that raising labour productivity depends on the application of new technologies. We must take effective steps to change the present situation in which the popularization and application of a large number of scientific and technological achievements have long been delayed. We must first of all overcome the conservative idea among some of our comrades of being content with things as they are, make greater efforts to publicize scientific and technological achievements and new techniques, seriously study and solve the problems that exist in the exchange and popularization of these achievements and change irrational regulations on keeping secrets.
>
> Close attention should be paid to the intermediate links between scientific research and industrial and agricultural production and essential pilot factories and workshops to trial-produce new products should be built or improved.
>
> We should study and formulate appropriate technical and economic policies and encourage the application of scientific and technological achievements. The standards by which production departments are examined should include the application of such achievements and the innovations made in technology. We should actively support their efforts to apply new techniques and improve work processes by providing them with the necessary materials and funds.

The elements of a thesis on innovation are contained in these three paragraphs. Fang attributed growth in labor productivity to technological innovation, but noted the existence of technical conservatism among "some of our comrades." To promote innovation, information about new technology and demonstrations of its efficacy on a pilot scale are necessary. There must also be an attempt to alter the motivations of microeconomic decision makers by incorporating criteria of innovativeness in evaluating the performance of "production departments" and by lessening the risks of innovation by providing "necessary materials and funds." How and by whom this general thesis on innovation will be operationalized remains to be seen.

It is notable, however, that a person in Fang Yi's position addressed the problem. China has shared some of the problems noted by Berliner[17] and has experimented with means designed to overcome organizational barriers separating research, production, and sales. Extensive efforts have been devoted to creating a mass culture of innovativeness.[18] Not all of these experiments have been successful, however, and the maintenance of the chain of innovation will be a continuing challenge to China's bureaucrats and managers.

The maintenance of the innovation chain is an institutional problem that must be solved if China is to realize the benefits of its investments not only in research and development, but also in foreign technology. Its maintenance will also be an important factor in sustaining political support for the ambitious new policies for science and technology.

In these first three chapters, I have attempted to describe China's new science policy, relate it to the goals of the four modernizations, identify its specific origins in the events of the past decade, and place it in a more general historical context.

The goals of the four modernizations entail particularly heavy demands on science and technology. To meet these, China's leaders have initiated a series of institutional reforms affecting the organization of science, planning, professional life, and research administration. In many ways, the reforms reestablished an institutional setting reminiscent of the pre–Cultural Revolution period. Moreover, the commitment to professionalism and internationalism in science and technology appeared to be stronger and less ambiguous than at any time since 1949. Nevertheless, there remained potential institutional constraints on scientific and technological development that will require a high order of leadership and administrative creativity to overcome. Chapter 4 examines two additional factors which will affect China's scientific progress.

Chapter Four

Manpower and Expenditures

The national development plans, including the plans for science and technology, which are reviewed in the previous chapters, are clearly quite ambitious. The realization or nonrealization of the plans will have a profound effect on the future of China. It is therefore useful to explore the human and financial resources available for these plans and identify any serious resource constraints. The following discussion focuses on scientific and technical manpower availability and on expenditures for science and technology.

MANPOWER

The manpower question is one which a number of Western visitors to and observers of China have identified as perhaps the major constraint on scientific development. This judgment is largely a qualitative one based upon the presumed effects of the disruptions suffered by the educational system from 1966 to 1976. Although this Western judgment is probably correct and indeed was confirmed consistently throughout 1977 and 1978 by the Chinese themselves, it is important to remember that in China technical manpower comes both from the educational system and from the ranks of workers and peasants who lack formal education. China seems to have been successful in recruiting technical manpower from the latter category, especially to engineering positions. Although promotion through the ranks unquestionably has been an important recruitment device for engineering manpower, by the late seventies it was no longer an adequate substitute for formal higher education in engineering given China's aspirations for both imported and indigenously developed technology.

It is also important to recall that reasonably complete and reliable manpower data have been unavailable outside of China since before the Cultural Revolution. As a result, there has been no comprehensive and systematic analysis of the manpower question since the pioneering efforts of the 1960s.[1] Indeed, it appears that reliable manpower data may not exist in China either. According to a June 23, 1978 New China News Agency report, the State Planning Commission, the State Scientific and Technological Commission, the Ministry of Civil Affairs, and the State Statistical Bureau had recently announced a decision to conduct a "nationwide survey of the existing scientific and technological personnel" . . . "in order to gain a comprehensive understanding of their numbers, levels of schooling, distribution and employment."[2]

In spite of these uncertainties we can make some gross estimates of trained manpower that may not be too far wrong. However, we also lack some of the more interesting contextual information that would give greater meaning to the gross figures. For instance, if China has a technical manpower shortage, how severe is it and where does it show up? What has been the output of training programs in different fields? Where have technically trained college graduates been employed, and what criteria have been used in employment decisions? What are the generational differences within the total technical manpower pool? Our ability to answer these questions is unfortunately rather limited. Nevertheless, the importance of the subject warrants an attempt to at least sketch the rough dimensions of the problem China's leaders confront.

We know that the manpower question has troubled China's leaders at least since 1975. As noted in chapter 1, the preparation of the "Outline Report" led to a fourfold categorization of China's scientific and technical personnel based upon age and place of training. Moreover, Fang Yi said that the number of research workers in a country of China's size should be several times greater than it is. At the National Science Conference, he called for an increase in the number of professional research workers to 800,000 by the year 1985. If one assumes that in 1979 the number was approximately 200,000, an increase to 800,000 would of course be an increase of "several times."[3]

Unfortunately, it is not clear what Fang Yi meant by professional research worker. For the moment, let us assume he meant trained scientists, engineers, and technicians employed in research and development. It is also unfortunate that the exact meaning of the 200,000 base figure is ambiguous, although this figure is quite close to the estimate made by Orleans in 1967.[4] Orleans calculated that at that time the total number of people employed in Chinese research and development was 425,000, of which approximately one-half were nontechnical personnel (see table 1).

It is unlikely that this number, if correct, would have changed significantly between 1967 and 1978. Considering additions and attritions in the manpower pool, we can assume a figure of 225,000 technical personnel in research and development for 1978. Orleans's estimate for the pre–Cultural

TABLE 1
TECHNICAL PERSONNEL, 1967

| | Place of Employment | | | |
Category	Higher Education	CAS	Other Sectors	Total
Scientists	1,500	2,000	25,000	27,500
Engineers	4,000	1,500	20,000	25,500
Technicians*				160,000
Total	5,500	3,500	45,000	213,000

*Deduced from the number of scientists and engineers using a 3:1 ratio.

Revolution period is the least conservative of standard Western estimates, and for the Chinese to reach 800,000 by 1985 from these other base figures would involve increases of more than several times.

The figures for research and development personnel should be considered in the context of the total scientific and technical manpower pool. Here again we can rely on Orleans's estimates cited in chapter 1. Orleans calculated that as of mid-1975 the total number of scientific and technical personnel who had completed higher education stood at approximately 1,300,000, including 725,000 engineers (55.8 percent of the total) and 575,000 scientists (44.2 percent) of whom some 180,000 were in agriculture and 240,000 were in medicine.[5]

If this figure is adjusted for 1978, assuming an average of 70,000 new graduates per year in science and engineering between 1975 and 1977, the estimated number of individuals in the manpower pool who had completed higher education is 1,450,000. Given these estimates for 1978, what is the likelihood of China having 800,000 professional research workers by 1985?

This question can be approached by calculating the ratio of research and development personnel to total science and technology graduates and by estimating the capacity of the higher educational system. Based upon Orleans's estimates, we can assume that the percentage of technical personnel engaged in research and development is approximately 15.5 percent of those who are college graduates in science and engineering. If that proportion remains constant through 1985, then the total number of scientists and engineers who are college graduates will be approximately 5,161,290 if the goal of 800,000 research workers is achieved. This number would result in an increase of 3,711,290 over the 1978-base estimate of 1,450,000.

Can China's educational system produce such a large number of graduates by 1985? To answer this question, let us assume with Orleans that the number of graduates in 1975 was 50,000 (almost all in science and engineering), a figure already considerably below the peak number of graduates in the pre—Cultural Revolution period. Reasonably reliable data from the year

1962–63 indicate that there were some 200,000 graduates in that year.[6] Of these, some 129,000 (nearly 65 percent) were in the fields of engineering, natural science, agriculture and forestry, and medicine. Assuming a modest increase in the total number of graduates to 250,000 by 1966–67 and that distribution by field remained the same, we can infer that the peak output of graduates in the sciences and engineering before the Cultural Revolution was 157,500. Let us further assume that this represented the educational system operating at full capacity.[7] It is then clear that the number of graduates produced in 1975, if Orleans is correct, represents only one-third to one-half of the output capacity of the educational system.

How soon can the pre–Cultural Revolution capacity be reattained? Since the reintroduction of examinations in late 1977, two classes have matriculated. The first numbered 278,000 and the second, admitted in October 1978, 290,000, and the total enrollment was more than 850,000.[8] With the extension of university training to four years, these figures indicate that pre–Cultural Revolution numbers of graduates will be surpassed in 1982.

Table 2 is a projection of the number of graduates between 1976 and 1985 based on figures of 50,000 for 1975, 278,000 for 1982, and 290,000 for 1983 (assuming no attritions and assumptions of a 10 percent increase per annum after 1983, and that 70 percent of the graduates will be in science or engineering).

This total of 1,415,330 is far below the estimated 3,711,290 required if the 15.5 percent ratio of research and development personnel to total science and technology graduates is to hold. The inconsistency raises doubts about a number of the assumptions made. First, the base figures could be wrong. Although the base figures are questionable, they are if anything on the high side and probably are not the main source of the discrepancy. Second, the estimates of the output capacity of the educational system may be wrong. To be sure, these are rough estimates that may underestimate a capacity for rapid expansion. On the other hand, the estimates of the annual number of graduates from 1976 to 1981 may be too generous. The margins of error here, however, again would not be sufficiently great to account for the discrepancy.

The most likely source of error concerns the relationship between research and development personnel and the total number of graduates in science and engineering. One possible problem might be that the initial ratio is not correct. Again, let us assume that it is, but that it need not remain so. A more likely explanation is that the ratio of 1975 will not remain the same through 1985. If these educational output estimates are roughly correct, the total number of individuals who are college graduates in science and engineering in 1985 should be around 2.5 million, if we allow for attrition. This would mean that if China is to reach the number of 800,000 professional research workers, the ratio of research and development personnel to total college

TABLE 2
COLLEGE GRADUATES, 1976–85
(Projected)

Year	All Fields	Science and Engineering
1976	107,100*	74,970
1977	116,900*	81,830
1978	120,000	84,000
1979	125,000	87,500
1980	140,000	98,000
1981	175,000	122,500
1982	278,000	194,600
1983	290,000	203,000
1984	319,000	223,300
1985	350,900	245,630
Total	2,021,900	1,415,330

*Based on figures on new entrants for 1973–74 and 1974–75 cited by Marianne Bastid-Bruguiere, "Higher Education in the People's Republic of China," in Organization for Economic Cooperation and Development, ed., *Science and Technology in the People's Republic of China* (Paris: OECD, 1977), p. 121, and assuming an attrition rate of 30 percent for those classes only.

graduates in science and engineering will be approximately 32 percent. This would mean a more intensive use of scientific and technical manpower in research and development and less intensive use elsewhere.

Another assumption made about the 800,000 figure is that it represents research and development personnel as understood by Orleans. As such, the figure represents slightly less than a fourfold expansion over Orleans's estimate of 213,000 for 1967. However, only about 25 percent (53,000) of those were scientists and engineers, who, it may be assumed for the moment, were college graduates (as opposed to many technicians and "worker engineers" who are not). If the interpretation of Fang Yi's target is changed to mean 800,000 *college-graduated scientists and engineers engaged in research*, then this represents an enormous increase in such manpower (approximately 750,000 over eight years). This would mean that more than one-half of the new graduates in science and engineering would be absorbed into research and development if no pre-1976 graduates were reassigned to research and development. This seems to be an inordinately high number given the demands for scientific and engineering personnel in nonresearch areas.

Without knowing what Fang Yi's target figure of 800,000 actually means, it is difficult to predict whether the educational system can respond to the demand for trained manpower. If the 800,000 figure is interpreted to include non–college-graduate technical support personnel and if the 3:1 ratio of support personnel to scientists and engineers holds, then it is reasonable to expect that the educational system will produce an additional 150–170,000 graduates of institutions of higher education for research and development out of a total estimate of 1,415,330 graduates by 1985. (In the following discussion, this is called Interpretation One.) If, as is more likely, Fang Yi meant that the total research and development force by 1985 would consist of 800,000 college graduates in science and engineering (from an assumed base of 50–60,000 in 1977), then according to my analysis, the educational system will have difficulty meeting this target (Interpretation Two). Again, one must recognize the possible errors in the data and assumptions underlying this analysis.

Although Interpretation One seems more feasible (i.e., training 10–20 percent of the total estimated graduates for research and development), when the quality of training is considered, even the attainment of this more modest goal raises some interesting issues.

One aspect of the manpower question that has engaged the attention of Western observers and has been discussed in China openly since 1975 is the question of the highly trained senior scientist, who is defined as capable of leading advanced training and research (a capability that is usually denoted in the West with the conferring of a doctorate).

The number of senior scientists China had in the early years of the People's Republic was painfully few. These were usually people who had studied abroad in the capitalist countries, often to the doctoral level, in the pre-Liberation or immediate post-Liberation period. This group numbered around 1,100 in 1962, according to Chu-yuan Cheng.[9]

An argument can be made that one of the most serious negative consequences of the Chinese adoption of a Soviet-style academy-centered science system was that the training potential of this group of 1,100 was underutilized. Had advanced research been based in the university, the argument continues, the senior scientists could have trained a far larger number of individuals who themselves would have been prepared to lead advanced training and research teams. Instead, many senior scientists were assigned to institutes of the CAS where their contact with advanced students was less (although not totally absent) and where much of their energy was channeled into administrative in addition to research tasks.

The visitor to Chinese research institutes and universities today still sees the influence of Western-trained senior scientists. Some of these individuals are rather old, and most occupy administrative positions of leadership. They are not typically found exercising direct, working leadership in the laboratories. Working leadership in the laboratories instead is exercised by individuals from the next two generations of scientists. These include three groups. The first group includes those trained in China before the Liberation; these typically graduated from well-known universities just prior to the Liberation, but did not study abroad. The second group consists of those who studied abroad in the Soviet Union or Eastern Europe, mainly during the 1950s. Members of these two groups belong to the same generation and are typically in their late forties and early fifties. The third group, generally the youngest, is made up of those who graduated in China after the Liberation and who sometimes (for those in the apparently more prestigious positions) had the benefit of advanced training in China.

It is from these three groups that much of the leadership for the modernization of science and technology must come. Together, they can be called the "new leadership corps" and must soon take over from the aging Western-trained group. It is difficult to estimate the size of the new leadership corps, but its importance warrants the attempt. In making this estimate, I assume that the new leadership corps will be drawn from two groups that can be identified on the basis of where they were trained.

The first such group are those who studied in the Soviet Union and other socialist countries. It has been estimated that approximately 15,500 scientists, "instructors," and graduate and undergraduate students were sent to the USSR for training from 1950–60.[10] Since not all the instructors and students were scientists, this number should be discounted. On the other hand, if those in science and engineering who studied in Eastern Europe are included, the commonly used figure of 10–11,000 individuals trained in science and engineering in the socialist countries is reached. However, not all of these returned to China to begin careers in research.

Four hundred of these Soviet-bloc-trained scientists and engineers received doctorate or candidate degrees,[11] and it can be assumed that they entered research and are qualified to become senior scientists. Of those who went to the USSR, 1,200 went as instructors and 5,500 went as undergraduates.[12] Most of these probably did not enter research. Twenty-three hundred went as scientists and graduate students,[13] including the 400 who received doctorates. If out of the remaining 1,900, 1,000 entered research and development and are now prepared to assume leadership positions, this yields a total of 1,400 potential senior scientists.

The second group can be defined as those who graduated from institutions of higher education in China, either just before or after the Liberation, and who received graduate training in China. A recent report stated that between 1,000 and 3,000 research students were admitted annually for graduate training at research institutes between 1949 and 1966.[14] If the average figure of 2,000 per year over this sixteen-year period is used, this yields a figure of some 32,000 who had some graduate training.

We may be able to get some idea of the number of research leaders from this group from the following considerations. From 1950–56, graduate training in China focused mainly on preparation for college teaching.[15] Let us assume then that 2,000 individuals at most, who had graduate training during this initial period, entered research and development.

From the time it was established in 1958 until the Cultural Revolution, the elite University of Science and Technology graduated some 8,000 students, including 1,600 per year from 1961 to 1965.[16] Let us assume that most of those from the classes of 1961, 1962, and 1963 ($n = 4,800$) completed graduate training before the disruptions of the Cultural Revolution and entered research and development. In addition to this 4,800, let us then assume that from 1957 to 1966, another 15,200 individuals received graduate training.[17] This brings the number of purely Chinese-trained members of the new leadership corps to 22,000. If the 1,400 largely Soviet-trained individuals are added, the total is 23,400.

If to this number are added the remainder of the Science and Technology University graduates ($n = 3,200$), plus another possible 3,000 who had some graduate or research apprentice experience since the beginning of the Cultural Revolution, there are approximately 30,000 members in the new leadership corps. It can be postulated that members of this group and approximately 700 members of the first generation lead research in institutes and lead research and give advanced instruction in universities.

How problematic is the size of this group for the tasks China has set for itself? If we assume there are approximately 100 institutes in the CAS and add to these the 88 key institutions of higher education that have been singled out for priority attention and some 200 major research institutes (there are probably more) from the ministerial sector (including the production ministries, the Academies of Medical Science and of Agriculture and of Forestry, and the defense sector), the total is 388 key centers of science and technology. These will make the greatest demands for advanced manpower. They probably will also be engaged in advanced training in addition to research and development. An equal allocation of personnel from the leadership corps would mean about 77 individuals per installation.

However, the members of the leadership corps are not equally distributed. According to Orleans's sectoral distribution of 53,000 scientists and engineers in 1967, approximately 6.5 percent were employed in the CAS, 8.5 percent in higher education, and 85 percent in the ministerial sector. If this distribution pattern holds for 1979, it results in about 1,950 members of the new leadership corps in the CAS (20 per institute), 2,550 in institutions of higher learning (30 per key university), and 25,500 in the ministerial sector.

It seems clear that even with the continuing contributions of the first generation, the demands on the new leadership corps for performance in research and teaching and increasingly for administration could be very taxing. For instance in teaching, based on the easier Interpretation One of

Fang Yi's 800,000 figure, some 18,750 college graduates per year must be trained for research and development work.[18] This in itself seems a manageable task for the new leadership corps. However, based on the more likely Interpretation Two, perhaps as many as 750,000 individuals over a period of eight years (93,750 per year) would have to be trained. This seems a heavy burden for an educational system with only 2,550 people in leadership positions.

There is, however, another important component of Chinese manpower plans: the reintroduction of graduate programs in universities, the institutes of the CAS, and some of the institutes in the ministerial sector. These programs were scheduled to offer a three-year course of advanced study leading to an independent research project and thesis. By autumn, 1978, some 9,000 postgraduates were to be enrolled in both the natural and social sciences.[19]

Sigurdson noted plans at Qinghua and Zhongshan universities to have as many as 5,000 and 1,000 graduate students, respectively, enrolled by 1985.[20] If one projects the Zhongshan figure for all 88 key universities, there will be 88,000 graduate students in universities, plus perhaps 5,000 in the CAS (50 per institute × 100 institutes). This graduate program will place additional demands on the new leadership corps. If the graduate student to instructor ratio is 5:1, approximately 20,000 individuals capable of leading and conducting graduate study will be required by 1985.

The discussion thus far has focused on the question of high-level manpower capable of leading research and advanced training. Since China lost more than ten years of advanced training, political leaders could not delay educational reforms any longer. The analysis here suggests that China will have difficulty meeting its educational and training goals and will continue to experience a manpower shortage for the short term. The analysis suggests that given the size of new leadership corps, the highest-priority utilization of high-level manpower over the next eight years should be given to education and advanced training, rather than to research and development. This analysis also suggests that a strong case can be made that China would profit significantly by sending as many as 10–20,000 students and scientists abroad for graduate and postdoctoral training during the next eight years. The Chinese of course have made arrangements with the United States and other countries to send Chinese students and scholars abroad for training. Interestingly, in public discussions of these arrangements, the figure of 10,000 has often been used as a target for 1985.[21] This move to seek overseas educational opportunities will lessen the training pressures on the new leadership corps and is the most expeditious way to increase the size of that leadership group.

Another aspect of the manpower question concerns the nonresearch and noneducational demands for scientists and particularly for engineers. The engineer as Sigurdson so nicely puts it, is

> concerned with design, construction, and production and application of fundamental scientific knowledge to the problems of the physical world. Under the direction of engineers, technicians of various types supervise/perform a wide range of field operations in production and construction, testing and development, installing and running engineering plants, drafting and designing products, estimating costs and selling and advising customers on the use of engineering or scientific equipment.[22]

Given the ambitious goals set in Hua Guofeng's speech cited in chapter 1, the demand for trained manpower in industry and agriculture will be high. Indeed, Fang Yi has mentioned the need to "train a professional contingent of several million people whose level is above that of university graduates."

Sigurdson recently explored the relation between increases in the number of engineers and industrial output in China.[23] Based on a recent Indian study, he hypothesized that the ratio of industrial output to number of engineers decreases as an economy expands. Sigurdson's data seem to support this relation in the Chinese case for the period 1957 to 1967. Indeed, the ratio drops so rapidly for the early 1960s that Sigurdson speculated that there may have been a surplus of engineers just before the Cultural Revolution. By the early 1970s, the value of the ratio began to increase, which suggested to Sigurdson that it was only at that point that the supply of manpower became problematic. Hence he tentatively concluded that the surplus that existed before the Cultural Revolution compensated for the loss of manpower during the late 1960s.

The relationship between industrial output and number of engineers is one of considerable potential importance in national manpower analyses. Far more comparative data over different stages of development are needed, however, before any significant conclusions about the relationship can be drawn. Nevertheless, the relationship can give us some idea of the probable need for engineers in China over the next decade. Table 3 illustrates the growth in demand for engineers through 1990, based on a constant output/ engineer ratio, a 10 percent per year growth in industrial output, and Orleans's estimate of 725,000 engineers in 1975.

Table 3 indicates about a fourfold increase in demand by 1990. This estimate of the demand for engineers may, however, be too conservative. First, Sigurdson's hypothesis is probably correct, and China will over this period probably experience a decrease in the output/engineer ratio. The plans for the four modernizations certainly seem to be increasingly engineer intensive. As a result, it would not be surprising if the demand for engineers by 1990 were nearer four to five million, rather than three million.

TABLE 3
GROWTH IN DEMAND FOR ENGINEERS

Year	Number of Engineers (Cumulative)	Annual Increase (Per Year)
1975	725,000	
1976	797,500	72,500
1977	877,250	79,750
1978	964,975	87,725
1979	1,061,473	96,498
1980	1,167,620	106,147
1981	1,284,382	116,762
1982	1,412,820	128,438
1983	1,554,102	141,282
1984	1,709,512	155,410
1985	1,880,463	170,951
1986	2,068,509	188,046
1987	2,275,360	206,851
1988	2,502,896	227,536
1989	2,753,186	250,290
1990	3,028,505	275,319

Second, China is already under-engineered. This is clear at most indus-trial plants one visits in China. In 1978, at the modern Shanghai Petro-chemical Works, for instance, there were only 20–30 college-graduate en-gineers; management claimed they could use 1,000. Only one out of three requests to the state for more engineers was met, however. Although the Shanghai Petrochemical Works may be atypical, it serves to make the general point that China lacks engineers, and for this reason as well, the estimates contained in table 3 may be too conservative.

These considerations again point out the need for the expansion of China's educational system. The peak total enrollment in higher education in the pre–Cultural Revolution period was approximately 965,000 in 1960–61,[24] and the largest number of graduates in engineering in any one year was probably the 77,000 in 1962–63.[25] If the supply of engineering manpower is to keep up with or surpass the pace of economic growth, the pre–Cultural Revolution figure had to be surpassed at least by 1978. After this year, the demands for manpower can be expected to tax increasingly the educational system unless the latter expands quickly. Such expansion will not only re-quire major capital investment, but also will place demands on the existing pool of manpower, demands which are potentially in conflict with demands for research and development and the training of an expanded pool of research and development workers. This again suggests that in the short run—until 1985—the highest-priority utilization of scientific and technical manpower may be in education rather than research.

Fang Yi not only spoke of a "professional contingent of several million people," he also noted the importance of a "mighty contingent of non-professional scientists and technicians" and the need to rely on both contingents for the four modernizations. While professional education languished during the past twelve years, much public support and praise went to the various innovative programs developed during the Cultural Revolution that offered training opportunities to workers and peasants. Despite the inconsistency between many aspects of the new policy and the policies of the Cultural Revolution, it is significant that such Cultural Revolution programs as the "July 21" and "May 7" workers' colleges are to be continued and expanded.[26] The July 21 workers' colleges are run by localities, factories, and mines and are intended to upgrade the technical knowledge of the industrial labor force. In addition, there are communist labor universities which, like the May 7 colleges, are oriented more toward the countryside; various spare-time educational programs; and on-the-job technical training. Reportedly, by the summer of 1976, there were 15,000 active July 21 and May 7 colleges with 780,000 students.[27]

Although these nonprofessional programs could probably benefit from an infusion of influence from the professional schools and although they are no substitute for programs of professional education, as they were apparently intended to be during the Cultural Revolution, the importance of these nonprofessional programs should not be underestimated. The existence of such programs and the motivation among workers to take advantage of them has contributed to the creation of a work force possessing considerable technical competence. Any visitor to a modern industrial complex in China containing only a handful of college-educated professional engineers can attest to this.

EXPENDITURES FOR SCIENCE AND TECHNOLOGY

Budgetary and expenditure data are among the more crucial kinds of information for assessing a nation's efforts in science and technology, but our knowledge of these matters in China is, unfortunately, very shallow. Until recently, China has not published any good data on expenditures for science since the 1950s. As a result, estimates of Chinese expenditures are based on a weak data base, and their compilation has involved considerable methodological license. For almost ten years, most Western observers considered it futile to even attempt to make such estimates. A recent effort by Billgren and Sigurdson is a welcome venture away from this pattern of caution.[28]

The Billgren and Sigurdson approach roughly follows the methodology of the last major effort at arriving at an estimate, that of Orleans in 1967. In the absence of reliable budget data, including budget categories and amounts per category, Orleans had to approach the problem in a different way. He

TABLE 4
RESEARCH AND DEVELOPMENT EXPENDITURES BY MAJOR CATEGORIES
1973

Category	Expenditures (billion yuan)	Percentage
Basic research	0.11	2.4
Agriculture and natural resources, excluding energy	0.81	18.0
Medicine and public health	0.52	11.0
Defense	1.00	22.0
Manufacturing, energy, and transportation	2.15	47.0
Total	4.59	100.0

SOURCE: Boel Billgren and Jon Sigurdson, "An Estimate of Research and Development Expenditures in the People's Republic of China in 1973." Industry and Technology occasional paper no. 16 (Paris: OECD Development Center, July, 1977), p. 7.

chose to focus on manpower estimates where the data base was somewhat stronger and on the wage structure for technical manpower. He then calculated a total wage bill for research and development, assumed that wages would constitute 40 percent of the research and development budget, and arrived at the figure of 1.35 billion yuan for 1965.[29]

Billgren and Sigurdson followed the same general approach for the year 1973. They made upward revisions in the total number of technical personnel and attempted to make allowances for changes in the structure of the economy since the start of the Cultural Revolution. As a result of their efforts, Billgren and Sigurdson came up with a research and development expenditures figure of 4.59 billion yuan (see table 4).[30] This figure is approximately U.S. $2.26 billion (at 2.03 yuan to the dollar) and represents about 1 percent of China's GNP in 1973.

An alternative approach to estimating Chinese expenditures on science and technology is found in a study conducted by Yuan-li Wu and Robert Sheeks. Although the findings are somewhat dated, the methodology followed calls attention to some of the possible faults in the Billgren and Sigurdson estimates. Wu and Sheeks worked with budget data from the 1950s. In their attempts to interpret that data and extrapolate from it to the 1960s, they were drawn into a discussion of budget categories, a topic which was neglected by Billgren and Sigurdson. It is clear that Wu and Sheeks were discussing a "science and technology budget," which is somewhat greater than the research and development budget alone. As a result of their calculations, Wu and Sheeks conjectured a budget of 4 billion yuan for 1965 (see table 5).[31]

Of interest here is the roughly 1 billion yuan figure for the Ministry of Defense, which is the same as Billgren and Sigurdson's figure for defense in

TABLE 5
SCIENCE AND TECHNOLOGY BUDGET
1965

Source	Distribution of Funds (percentage)	Value (billion yuan)
Science budget*	33	1.3
Government production ministries	35	1.4
Ministry of Defense	25	1.0
Local governments and production enterprises	7	0.3
Total	100	4.0

*The science budget is part of the general budget for social, cultural, and educational expenditures. Other major budget categories used by the government were those for economic construction, defense, administration, and "other." See Yuan-li Wu and Robert B. Sheeks, *The Organization and Support of Scientific Research and Development in Mainland China* (New York: Praeger Publishers, 1970), pp. 177, 179.

1973. In discussing budget categories, however, Wu and Sheeks called attention to the financing of military research and development and particularly the Chinese nuclear weapons program. They concluded that much of the funding for military research and development probably originated in the budgets of the production ministries and the science budget, as well as from the budget of the Ministry of Defense. The cost of the nuclear program alone in 1965, they concluded, was probably on the order of 2.2 billion yuan.[32]

It is not clear where Billgren and Sigurdson placed the nuclear program. If they intended to include it in the defense category, their figure of 1 billion yuan seems much too low for two reasons. The Chinese nuclear program has of course continued during the past ten years. Although the figure given by Wu and Sheeks for 1965 may have reflected a large amount of capital construction in the nuclear program that may no longer be required, it is unlikely that expenditures on nuclear weapons would in 1973 have been so much lower than the Wu and Sheeks 1965 estimate. In addition, China had in the interim begun missile and space programs, the greater share of which should be considered a defense-related expenditure. We have no data on expenditures in these fields, but a comparison with the Japanese space program may be instructive. The total Japanese space budget for 1976 was some U.S. $293.3 million,[33] or some 595 million Chinese yuan.[34] A conservative estimate of the cost of the Chinese missile and space programs in the early 1970s therefore might be 0.5 billion yuan. This again would be a substantial portion of the total research and development budget estimated by Billgren and Sigurdson, which unfortunately cannot be accounted for directly by their approach.

The discussion above indicates the difficulties foreign observers have had in estimating expenditures for science and technology in China. Based on assumptions different from those used by Billgren and Sigurdson, but which are reasonable on a prima facie basis nonetheless, the Billgren and Sigurdson estimates would appear to be too conservative. Most other countries with both types of programs were spending between 1.5 and 3 percent of GNP by 1970. It is difficult, to be sure, to compare China with these other countries without a number of qualifications. But if China is assumed to conduct programs in space and in nuclear weapons by spending less than 2 percent of GNP on research and development, say 1.75 percent instead, on a GNP of U.S. $216.75 billion for 1973, this would still mean a research and development budget of $3.79 billion or about 7.7 billion yuan.[35]

For the first time since the 1950s, China has made public selected state budget data.[36] The figures released seemingly invalidate the more liberal interpretation of Chinese expenditures, and are more consistent with the Billgren and Sigurdson estimate. The 1979 budget contains some 5.87 billion yuan for science and technology. This represents approximately 5.2 percent of the state budget, and is an increase of 10 percent over the 1978 budget. If we assume that China's GNP had grown to approximately 826 billion yuan by 1979, the budget for science and technology would amount to only about .7 percent of GNP, a figure considerably less than even the Billgren and Sigurdson interpretation would have led us to expect. This surprisingly low figure may be a further indication of the devastating effect the Cultural Revolution and post-Cultural Revolution reforms have had on Chinese science.

Given the statements of Chinese leaders concerning the role of science and technology in meeting the four modernizations, expenditures on science and technology can be expected to increase significantly in the near future. Two large items that can be expected to expand the budget quickly are a possible increase in the wage bill and definite increases in capital construction. The increase in the former would include an initial one-time spurt resulting from a large number of promotions and hence salary increases for professional personnel. All such promotions had been frozen for more than ten years, but are now being made. The number of individuals affected and the extent of the impact on the wage bill are difficult to determine. If an increase were applied across the board, it could amount to as much as 0.6 billion yuan. The increasing legitimation of material rewards, the rhetoric about the importance of professional personnel to China, and the planned increase in the number of professional personnel all indicate an expanding wage bill component in the national science budget.

The second item forcing expansion is capital construction. New institutes have been and are being added to the CAS, including two (in high energy physics and nuclear fusion) that promise to consume large amounts of resources. In addition, the planned increases in undergraduate and graduate enrollments will soon require expansion in university and CAS facilities. If the strengthening of such items of infrastructure as sophisticated information services are added, it becomes clear that the budget for science and technology will expand rapidly.

The human, financial, and institutional resources available for China's drive toward modernization are difficult to gauge with certainty. The greatest constraint on rapid progress is probably that imposed by shortages of trained manpower. The extent of the shortage and the distribution of its impact are, however, difficult to determine.

The capacity of the educational system is a constraint as well. The necessary expansion of the manpower pool required to meet the goals mentioned by Fang Yi have placed and will continue to place enormous demands on the educational system. Yet by early 1979, there were signs that the present educational system had reached the limits of its capacities. Total enrollment had swelled to 850,000, 180,000 more than the figure for 1965. Yet there were actually fewer facilities in 1979 than in 1965.[37] Thus, the 1979 retrenchment seen in economic policy generally, also was seen in the educational system, and it is unlikely that manpower targets can be met.

In the absence of more detailed budget data from China, it is difficult to estimate Chinese expenditures for science and higher education generally and research and development specifically. It seems likely that expenditures for research and development have been adequate in the past, but as suggested in this chapter, the modernization of science and technology will require substantial increases in research and development expenditures in the future. In the face of competing needs for state revenues, for instance in education, it is possible that funding will become a far more important constraint on scientific and technological development than it has been in the past.

China has an impressive, but by no means problem-free network of institutions for science and technology and much experience resulting from many years of institutional innovation. In concluding chapter 3, I suggested that the performance of these institutions will be an important factor affecting the acceptability of and support for the four modernizations program. The performance of China's institutions are critically dependent upon the availability of trained personnel to staff them, and financial resources to support them. Although a lack of data precludes a detailed assessment of China's human and financial resources, this chapter has indicated that shortages of both are serious constraints on scientific and technological development. China's new interests in international scientific and technological relations should be examined with these constraints in mind.

Chapter Five

◆━━◆

International Relations

The association between international political relations and international scientific and technological relations is an ambiguous one. Western scientists participating in international scientific affairs often emphasize the value of scientific contacts for enhancing international understanding. These contacts are seen as a means for improving international relations, at times despite unfavorable political relations. Policymakers and administrators on the other hand sometimes regard the position of the scientists as somewhat naive. From the viewpoint of the policymaker, scientific relations follow political relations and can flourish only after a political framework has been established.

Although my own bias is toward the latter position, it is not my purpose to defend it here. My purpose instead is to raise the issue of the ambiguity and the complexity of the relation between political and scientific ties. In the case of Chinese-American relations, for instance, the Shanghai Communiqué provided a framework for limited Sino-American scientific contacts. Once the contacts were established, one might argue that they helped improve relations between the two countries in the face of six years of stagnated political relations. Such an argument would probably be correct.

One might also raise the question of the political consequences of scientific relations. As noted earlier in this report, it is both theoretically likely and, according to the Chinese, factually true that increased numbers of foreign scientists coming to China, including Americans after 1972, contributed to the identification of serious problems in China's research and development efforts. In particular, comments about the neglect of basic research did apparently influence the thinking of political leaders and contribute to the major redirection of science policy discussed in this report. As I pointed out in an earlier paper, it is also theoretically likely that Chinese scientists by traveling abroad and receiving foreign scientists in China will alter their images of scientific work and the means required to complete it.[1] These alterations are in turn likely to be converted into demands on and requests and advice to the government for adjustments in science policy.

MODES OF INTERNATIONAL INTERACTIONS
IN SCIENCE AND TECHNOLOGY

International scientific and technological relations should also be viewed as they are in China, as an important means of overcoming constraints inhibiting national scientific and technological objectives. In the contemporary world, this aspect of international relations manifests itself in the international technology-transfer phenomenon and in numerous cooperative agreements among nations to share costs, particularly in expensive areas of research. The recipient's motivation for engaging in a technology-transfer relationship is usually the desire to leapfrog intermediate stages of technological development. The desire is to effect the commercial operation of reasonably advanced machinery and processes beyond domestic production capabilities. The conditions for affecting successful transfers are not usually fully understood and during the last ten years, many students of development have expressed serious reservations about the economic, social, and political appropriateness of much of the technology being transferred. By 1979, these questions were being asked about China as well following the surge of Chinese interest in advanced technology during 1978.

The most spectacularly successful case of importing technology in order to bypass intermediate stages of technological development and achieve rapid increases in productivity and product quality is, of course, the post–World War II Japanese case.[2] Although our understanding of this case remains incomplete, aspects of it suggest that many of the commonly held assumptions about technology-transfer efforts are wrong. In the context of this report, one of the most important of these lessons is that technology transfer cannot substitute for an underdeveloped, indigenous research and development capability. The Japanese case suggests that a reasonably well-developed research and development capability, including adequate numbers of scientific and technical personnel with reasonably high levels of training, is a prerequisite for successful transfer. Such a capability seems particularly important for (1) achieving a degree of independence from foreign technology suppliers in defining technical needs; (2) reaching informed decisions, again with a measure of independence, on the quality and availability of world technology; and (3) adapting foreign technology to indigenous needs and rapidly improving on it. The Japanese case also suggests that a successful major technology-import program generates indigenous research and development, although the research and development is "absorptive" and "renovative" rather than innovative. Reportedly, in some areas of technology, as much as 80 percent of Japanese industrial research and development expenditures went for such absorptive or renovative purposes between 1950 and 1966.[3] Thus, technology importation does not necessarily stultify indigenous research and development, although it can have a formative influence on a nation's scientific and technological development.

A second type of international scientific and technological relationship serving national aspirations is the cooperative project involving cost sharing. These projects have been concluded by a number of industrialized nations, either on a bilateral or on a multilateral basis, in areas of research involving high costs, great uncertainties, or special types of research complementarities. Cooperation in the fields of space, high energy physics, and energy research and development are ready examples.

The final category of international scientific and technological relations is conducted through international organizations. The International Council of Scientific Unions (ICSU) and its member unions in various disciplines are the most important in the field of science. In technology, there are numerous U.N.-affiliated and non–U.N.-affiliated organizations for such functional areas as meteorology, telecommunications, health, and environmental protection.

The variety of international scientific and technological relations can be categorized in yet another way. In principle, relations can be conducted on professional (typically, scientist to scientist, scientific organization to scientific organization), commercial, and governmental levels. Indeed, various combinations of these exist in the world of international science and technology. However, given China's socialist system and the absence of relatively autonomous commercial and professional sectors, governmental interests influence international scientific and technological relations in major ways, and mold commercial and professional relations in ways unknown in capitalist societies. Nevertheless, it is useful to maintain this three-level distinction as long as the primacy of political considerations in China is kept in mind.

THE PATTERN OF PAST SCIENTIFIC AND TECHNOLOGICAL RELATIONS

China's approach to international science and technology has been consistently to "put politics in command." International relations in science and technology are intended to serve political purposes and are conducted within a political framework. The Chinese government has used science and technology as tools of diplomacy and has entered into scientific and technological relations in order to facilitate the achievement of national development goals. The latter activity claims most of our attention at present, but the former should not be overlooked.

China's international scientific relations can also be categorized in terms of the countries and organizations with which relations are maintained and the types of agreements governing those relationships. Throughout the 1950s, of course, China's relations were mainly with the Soviet Union and East European nations. They were a consistent part of an overall foreign policy stance of "leaning to one side." In addition, these relations were expected to, and did in important ways, contribute to China's national development objectives. Apart from the large amount of industrial technology that came to China as a result of these ties, these relations also gave China access to reasonably advanced scientific instrumentation and opportunities for advanced training for a generation of scientists. In addition, these relations did much to shape the institutional structure of Chinese science and technology. Indeed, trained manpower and the institutional structure are important legacies of this period for contemporary China.

Relations with Soviet-bloc countries were typically the products of two kinds of agreements. The first type was a bilateral government-to-government agreement for cooperation across a broad range of topics in applied science and technology. The aim usually was to spur cooperation between various ministries of the two countries, and the agreement was coordinated through a joint committee for scientific and technological cooperation. The committees would meet at least once every two years to reaffirm the enabling agreement and make plans for subsequent cooperation.

Because of the importance of a central academy of sciences in the Soviet system, the relations of the 1950s also included academy-to-academy agreements, which were more clearly in the area of science as opposed to technology. In addition, the 1950s also saw multilateral agreements among the socialist countries, perhaps the best known of which is the agreement for cooperation in physics using the facility at Dubna.

The relations between China and the USSR were of special importance. Importations of Soviet technology were carefully coordinated with Chinese economic development plans. Large numbers of Soviet scientific and technical advisors were sent to China, and China's plans for scientific development were reviewed by Soviet scientists and administrators and included provisions for Soviet cooperation and assistance.

Although problems in Sino-Soviet scientific and technological relations are not normally cited as contributing to the Sino-Soviet split, there are many indications that those relations were far from harmonious. When political relations began to deteriorate, the scientific and technical relations had not created a fund of understanding and goodwill that could be used to sustain the political relations, despite the fact that the withdrawal of Soviet assistance created many new problems for the Chinese economy and for Chinese science.

As Sino-Soviet relations deteriorated, China began in the 1960s to import selectively technology from Japan and Western Europe and to send a limited number of Chinese students to noncommunist countries for training. However, the lack of diplomatic relations with many capitalist countries at this time, the presence of Taiwan in many international science organizations, and the doctrine of self-reliance limited the expansion of scientific and technological relations. Notable exceptions, however, were relations with third-world countries, with whom China shared many problems of scientific development and whose political favors China courted as part of the growing Sino-Soviet rivalry. Of interest in this regard are two international symposiums China hosted in 1964 and 1966, which, although not exclusively for third-world nations, were nevertheless strongly oriented toward them.

The Cultural Revolution with its expanded emphasis on self-reliance and its nativist, anticosmopolitan, and strongly antiprofessional themes significantly reduced international scientific contacts and technological relations. But it may also have contributed to an understanding of the limits of self-reliance, for as China entered the 1970s, extreme insistence on self-reliance gave way to the idea of "making things foreign serve things Chinese." This change in emphasis paralleled China's reentry into more conventional international affairs following the Cultural Revolution and, importantly, China's admission to the United Nations. The early 1970s saw an expansion of interest in foreign technology and an increased number of scientific visitors from abroad.

However, as was true in the immediate pre–Cultural Revolution period, international scientific and technological contacts again became an issue in Chinese domestic politics. Zhou Enlai and his supporters were prepared to expand the importation of foreign technology and scientific contacts with the capitalist countries; the Gang of Four apparently opposed these moves. In part the issue was self-reliance, and in part it concerned the strategy of using Chinese raw materials as the chief means of paying for imported technology, a strategy the Gang of Four allegedly felt would reduce China to semicolonial status.

The removal of the Gang of Four has opened up what now seems to be a new era in China's international scientific and technological relations. China entered this new era with a wealth of experience garnered from the age of Sino-Soviet cooperation during the 1950s, the period of extreme self-reliance in the late 1960s, and the recent era of association with capitalist countries. These past experiences seem to have shaped the new posture into one of pragmatism and flexibility, designed to use international contacts to help overcome domestic constraints on development without becoming dependent. The expansion of interest in and contacts with foreign science and technology was, however, remarkably rapid after the purge of the Gang of Four, and a number of questions remain about the long-term impact of these contacts.

INTERNATIONAL SCIENTIFIC AND TECHNOLOGICAL RELATIONS AND THE FOUR MODERNIZATIONS

At the center of China's current interest in international science and technology are the potential contributions foreign contacts can make to the realization of the four modernizations. The immediate goal of course is to overcome technological gaps in agriculture, industry, and national defense by importing and deploying technology unavailable in China. Although we have seen and will continue to see significant increases in such imports, by 1979 certain factors had already imposed limits on this type of activity.[4]

The first of these concerns China's ability to pay for foreign technology. As we have seen, China has decided to expand its imports of foreign technology, but the scale and pace of such imports remain unclear as of 1979. Western euphoric expectations of 1978 about a vast Chinese market for technology were dampened by Chinese retrenchment policies in 1979 as a result of China's realization that the financial burden was becoming unmanageable. The Chinese have, however, signaled a willingness to break with past, rather conservative financial practices (such as reliance on relatively short-term credits in the form of deferred payments) and to seek more flexible financial arrangements. These include a commitment to expanded tourism, product payback schemes, use of development aid from both the United Nations and from national programs (e.g., the Japanese Overseas Economic Cooperation Fund), and the use of long-term loans and joint ventures.[5]

Japanese estimates based upon 1978 information suggest that China's foreign capital requirements for the period up to 1985 could be as high as U.S. $200 billion. To provide funds of this magnitude, Japanese commercial and financial circles have proposed the idea of an international "mini–Marshall Plan," in which Western governments acting in concert would offer China relatively low interest loan packages in order to encourage commercial banks to make syndicated loans.[6]

The scaling down of the four modernizations programs in 1979 raises doubts that this Japanese estimate accurately reflects China's short-term needs, and it is unlikely that China is willing to incur foreign obligations of that magnitude. For the purposes of this analysis, it is sufficient to note that China's leaders seem to be more willing than in the past to enter into foreign indebtedness with confidence that such debt need not lead to dependence. Instead, policy seems to be based on the realization that if managed properly, such debt can provide economic decision makers with considerably more flexibility. This changed position on foreign indebtedness, new efforts at export promotion, and the promise of increased export earnings from tourism, raw materials, and manufactures suggest that while the financing of imported technology will be a constraint on the development of technology-transfer relations, China's leaders hope to make it manageable.

It is important to note that Chinese trade with the nonmarket economies continues and offers China additional sources of technology. This trade represented 18 percent of China's total trade in 1976, with a value of U.S. $2.35 billion. This figure is comparable to the peak value of $2.98 billion in 1959 when trade with nonmarket economies represented 69 percent of China's foreign trade.[7] Moreover, this trade has been China's chief source of supply for "aircraft, electric power generating equipment, coal mining machinery, and land based oil drilling rigs."[8] The potential attractiveness of this trade to China and to its nonmarket partners is that it is largely conducted through commodity exchange agreements and thus does not involve significant expenditures of the hard currencies that are commonly in short supply in these economies.

A second type of limitation on increases in imported technology is China's ability to absorb and deploy foreign technology sensibly. There are a number of aspects to this question. First, China seems intent not only on using foreign technology, but also on learning from it. Indeed, the systematic study of imported technology is probably a precondition for avoiding dependence on foreign technology. However, both successful utilization and effective learning require skilled manpower, which—as we have seen—is in short supply. It is difficult to quantify this problem, but as suggested earlier in this chapter, the Japanese case is relevant. In pursuing its aggressive technology-import program in the post–World War II era, Japan had a highly literate population and a corps of engineers, managers, and scientists appropriate to its size and experience in industrial technology.

We have seen that manpower availability is perhaps the dominant constraint on China's domestic research and development. In the short run, it would seem to be a major constraint on a technology-import policy as well, manifesting itself both in shortages of the engineers needed to receive and operate foreign plants and equipment and of the research and development personnel needed to analyze and improve on foreign technology in order to gain maximum benefit from the import program. However, the manpower constraint on effective absorption of transferred technology may be eased somewhat by the availability of training services from foreign technology suppliers.[9]

A second aspect of the absorption/deployment question is what might be called the problem of achieving "systemic integration." A given piece of imported equipment or even an entire plant must be integrated with a larger pattern of economic activity if the full potential of the imported technology is to be realized. For instance, it makes little sense to import the capability to produce jet engines without also having the capability to design and build airframes.[10] I observed a typical example of the problem of systemic integration during a visit in May 1978 to a large, modern, imported urea plant at Daqing. The plant was operating at only one-third capacity due to a shortage of freight cars to move the product to end users. In other cases, ultramodern plants and equipment are not operating according to design specifications because of shortages of electric power.

Thus, technology imported as part of a solution may in turn create a problem in another part of the system. Since all such problems cannot be solved simultaneously, the Chinese will probably attempt to limit their occurrence. One way to do this would be to define priorities for imported technology and limit what is imported to that which can be integrated into a larger organizational network.

The foreign exchange, manpower, and systemic integration problems together indicate a more fundamental question concerning the importation of technology. As the proposed solution to the systemic integration problem illustrates, a "rational" solution to this problem is possible through systemic analysis and the setting of priorities. This, however, raises the question of who will do the analyses and set the priorities. In short, the decision-making process relating to foreign technology is a very important, yet inadequately understood factor in China's overall scientific and technological development.

There is no doubt that the Chinese realize the importance of this realm of decision making and, particularly, the importance of having an adequate informational base. Susan Swannack-Nunn reported that Chinese scientists serve as consultants to Chinese trading companies, and in a recent study of professional societies, Robert Boorstin demonstrated their role in providing technical counsel on technology-import decisions.[11] Chinese organizations interested in importing technology seem to be doing their homework before recommending decisions. During the last quarter of 1977, the Ministry of the Metallurgical Industry, for instance, in cooperation with the China Metals Society, convened a series of weekly seminars on the iron and steel industries in Japan and the United States and on the world's best iron-smelting, steel-refining, and steel-rolling technologies.[12]

Such organizations have been sending increasing numbers of delegations abroad to scout the state of technology in relevant fields. Reportedly these delegations are well prepared and show an enormous capacity for absorbing information. Upon returning, the delegations go through an extensive technical debriefing, which, in the case of a recent Petroleum Ministry group, involved the direct participation of the minister and vice-minister.[13]

The process of decision making regarding the acquisition of foreign technology needed in Chinese scientific research is illustrated by a recent report on the efforts of the CAS's Institute of Oceanography to procure an advanced research vessel.[14] This project is reportedly one of the top 25 priority items in the new science development plan. The decision-making process involved an initiative from the institute, approval from the academy, and authorization from the State Council. After less than one year of work, this first phase was completed in December 1977. With this high-level authorization, the institute began detailed studies of its objectives and of the domestic capabilities for reaching those objectives.[15] This led to the conclusion that the ship should be procured abroad. An interdisciplinary and interorganizational team was then formed to investigate the state of the art in Japan and the United States. The delegation was abroad for nearly six weeks. The recommendation of the team will require approval of the CAS, which in turn will pass it on to the Ministry of Foreign Trade and finally to the China National Machinery Import and Export Corporation, which will contact potential suppliers.

One of the interesting questions about the decision-making processes affecting foreign technology concerns what is now in the West called "policy analysis." To what extent are Chinese policies and decisions inspired, shaped, monitored, and evaluated by research groups engaged in systematic analysis? It is unclear how developed policy analysis is at present in China. However, the new interest in and legitimacy of the social sciences and the birth of social studies of science noted in chapter 1 lead one to expect that the various facets of technology transfers will soon be subject to an intellectual review one step removed from in-house staff analysis. Two possible centers of this activity are the Economic Research Institute of the new Chinese Academy of Social Sciences and the Economic Research Institute of the State Planning Commission.[16]

The thoroughness with which the Chinese are approaching the search for foreign technology is reminiscent of the Japanese case. The mere accumulation of good information is, however, no guarantee that priorities will be set wisely. Some economically rational mechanism for resolving conflicts over priorities is required. The Japanese case is again illustrative. Regardless of how one interprets the administrative guidance provided by the Ministry of International Trade and Industry (that is, how much there was and how good it was), it nevertheless seems true that the Japanese were able to set priorities and plan for systemic integration in their technology acquisition strategy. Although this decision-making process was by no means apolitical, narrow political interests offering no long-term economic or social benefits appear to have been generally checked, and political rationality was not entirely at variance with economic rationality.

It is rather difficult at this point to anticipate future politics of foreign technology in China. It seems for the moment that the highly charged symbolic politics of self-reliance as practiced by the Gang of Four may now be part of history. Instead the politics of foreign technology will likely become intersectoral distributive politics in which various vertical systems (such as production ministries and the branches of the military) will vie for relatively scarce opportunities to import technology. As the oceanographic research vessel case illustrates, there are multiple points in the decision-making process for competitive claims—both intraorganizational as well as interorganizational—to be made. Thus, in the competition for the means to procure foreign technology, there can be no guarantees that political rationality will mesh with economic rationality—China's socialist system and the best efforts of its planners notwithstanding.

A significant recent development relating to the problems of manpower, systemic integration, and decision making regarding foreign technology is China's decision to enter what are essentially foreign consultancy arrangements. Among the more significant are those dealing with core industries. An agreement reportedly has been made with the Mitsubishi Corporation, and discussions are now proceeding with the Fuyo Group. The catalogue of such consultancy agreements, or prospective agreements, also includes assistance for the development of railways (France, Japan), harbors (Denmark), mining (Germany), telecommuncations (Germany, France), energy (Germany, United States), metallurgy (Sweden, Australia, Japan), papermaking (Japan), petrochemicals (United States, Japan), and business management (Europe, Japan).[17]

China's interest in foreign technology presages significantly expanded international scientific and technological contacts. Such technology also offers many opportunities for China to achieve some of the many goals of the four modernizations. However, limitations on the means for paying for foreign technology, on trained manpower, and on the ability to make consistently sound decisions are all possible contraints on a technology-import strategy. The Chinese, however, appear to have given these problems considerable thought and are approaching the solutions flexibly and innovatively.

INTERNATIONAL SCIENTIFIC RELATIONS

China is also eagerly expanding international relations in science and learning more about scientific research in other countries. As noted earlier in this report, the peculiar history of science and technology in China since 1949 has resulted in an unequal distribution of levels of scientific and technological capabilities. In particular, basic research has been underemphasized, with the result that a strong basic research tradition was thwarted. More importantly, those scientists most capable of sustaining a basic research tradition are generally of the senior, now elderly, generation.

As Chinese leaders have come to reevaluate basic research, they are faced with shortages not only of trained manpower generally, but also of a special type of manpower—the experienced scientist capable of leading research and training, in what, in the final analysis, is a type of master-apprentice relationship.

Despite the dramatic expansion in China's international scientific contacts since 1977, the scope and depth of future scientific relations remains to be seen. In 1977 and 1978 we saw the beginnings of joint research by Chinese and foreign scientists and the sending of an increasing number of Chinese scientists and students abroad. These moves make a great deal of sense because they take advantage of foreign relations to compensate for weaknesses in training available in China. In particular, China is interested in advanced mid-career training for earlier graduates of Chinese universities who are prospective members of what I have called the "new leadership corps" and in graduate training for younger, more recent graduates.

In short, China's new use of international scientific relations offers a relatively economical and quick solution to the vexing manpower problems that we have observed in a number of contexts. The present course of action, however, marks a major change in government policy and in the social values underlying past policies. It is unclear whether these social values can be changed as quickly as policy, and there is therefore reason to suspend judgment on just how extensive and permanent the future participation of China's scientists in the international scientific community will be.

One important mechanism for facilitating international scientific and technological relations is the government-to-government agreement, including those involving scientific and technological cooperation between government agencies. As we have seen, China entered such agreements with all the Soviet-bloc countries in the 1950s, and some of these are still in force. Until recently, such agreements had not been concluded with technologically advanced capitalist nations.

However, by the end of 1977, a case could have been made that expanded cooperation would be in China's interest. Such cooperation would give China access to an expanded range of scientific and technical information, it could serve to set the pace or be the point of reference for Chinese research and development in certain fields, and it could ease the financial burden of an ambitious research and development program through cost-sharing arrangements.

Government-to-government arrangements are particularly important in utilizing international contacts to reach the objectives in the eight priority areas discussed in chapter 1. Profitable government-to-government relations could be envisioned in the areas of agriculture, energy, space, genetic engineering, and high energy physics, as well as in such important areas as health, environmental quality and environmental protection, seismology, and oceanography.

It is not surprising, therefore, that throughout 1978, China's scientific contacts with the governments of capitalist countries expanded. The first formal agreement with a Western country for scientific and technological cooperation was signed with France in January 1978. It called for increased exchanges over the next five years, joint research projects in the areas of genetics and medicinal plants, development of a scientific data bank, and joint study of tungsten resources.[18] In April, Fang Yi and the director of the West German Science Exchange Center discussed the expansion of scientific exchanges between the two countries,[19] and also in April, China signed an agreement for the use of a Franco-German satellite.[20] In October, an agreement providing for cooperation in energy, raw materials, aeronautics and space, physics, applied mathematics and information technology, agriculture, medicine, environmental protection, and ocean policy was signed with the West German Ministry of Research and Technology.[21]

A number of other scientific and technological contacts with nonsocialist countries were initiated in 1978. In what was probably the first meeting of its kind, an international symposium on plant-tissue culture, jointly sponsored by the CAS and the Australian Academy of Sciences in accordance with an interacademy agreement, was held in Beijing in May.[22] A major event in the development of Sino-American relations occurred in July when President Carter's science advisor, Dr. Frank Press, led a delegation composed of the heads of the major federal science agencies to China. The significance of this visit and subsequent developments following the normalization of relations between the two countries are assessed in the next chapter.

Entry into government-to-government scientific relations with nonsocialist countries—relations which Western industrialized nations enter almost routinely—marks a significant departure for China. The future development of these relations, particularly those calling for agency-to-agency cooperation, will be an indication of China's long-range thinking about modernization. Such relations entail the development of intimate partnerships between government agencies of two countries. China's willingness to enter into such cooperative arrrangements with governments of different social systems, which until recently were considered actually or potentially hostile, is of considerable political and scientific importance. Thus, the particulars of expanded government-to-government scientific and technological relations, especially those involving cooperation between government agencies, bear watching since they will provide indications of China's vision of the future world order.

As a result of the PRC's entry into the United Nations, it has replaced Taiwan in many U.N. functional agencies having science- or technology-related missions. By the end of 1978, the main area of international science where Chinese participation had not yet been secured was in the International Council of Scientific Unions and most of its member unions. Notable exceptions were the International Unions of Geological Sciences, Geodesy, and Geophysics, which voted to expel Taiwan and seat the People's Republic, and the International Union of Crystallography, which never included Taiwan among its members. The actions of the geoscience unions met with criticism, particularly from American scientists, and did not precipitate similar moves from other unions. As a result, the ICSU continued to search for a formula that would allow PRC participation without the complete ouster of Taiwan. At its October 1978 biennial assembly, it decided to explore further ways of achieving the participation of scientists from both sides of the Taiwan Strait.[23] Scientists from the two Chinas have begun to attend the same international meetings, and the ICSU therefore seemed to feel that possibilities existed for accommodating the interests of both sides. In addition, the normalization of relations between the United States and the PRC should make it somewhat less tenable for American scientists in the ICSU and its member unions to uphold the interests of Taiwan in quite the same way as they had in the past.

To summarize, China now seems prepared to enter the world of international science and technology more fully than at any time since 1949, including all three levels discussed at the beginning of this chapter. At the professional level, Chinese scientists are beginning to attend important international conferences and generally travel abroad more frequently. China has demonstrated a strong interest in increasing the number of individuals sent abroad for training and in expanding the areas of collaborative research. Foreign scientists are being invited to China for longer stays to give lectures, to visit research installations, and in some cases to assume professorial appointments. These changes mark an important step beyond the scientific tourism of the early and mid-1970s that played an important role in familiarizing foreign scientists with Chinese research, but which was necessarily superficial scientifically.

I have tried to develop an argument here as to why, given China's current goals, it appears rational to increase contacts at the professional level. The argument, however, is made from an American perspective in a milieu lacking the political symbolism of the recent Chinese past. Although the Chinese have also concluded that expanded contacts at the professional level are in their interests, it is not entirely clear how they plan to deal with their legacy of political symbols. Thus, we must not forget that active participation in international science at the professional level will entail an accommodation with cosmopolitanism and elitism and hence a significant change in those attitudes and values that have shaped Chinese science policy for almost thirty years.

At the commercial level also, one sees a high degree of interest in foreign technology and instrumentation that is a break from the practices of years past. China has clearly decided—for the moment at least—that the achievement of the four modernizations requires a substantial amount of foreign technology. It remains to be seen, however, just how much foreign technology will be imported, what kinds of terms such transactions will involve, and how China will prepare itself to absorb such technology. In spite of the large number, high monetary value, and variety of China's initiatives to acquire foreign technology during the past two years, there are some possible constraints, discussed above, on the scope of such an acquisition program.

At the intergovernmental level, the Chinese seem to realize that considerable benefit will accrue to them through expanded relations. Government-to-government relations facilitate relations at the professional and commercial levels. They carry their own benefits as well, particularly, but not exclusively in areas of "big" science and those involving complex technological missions, which as we have seen, are high on China's list of priorities.

THE LARGER POLITICAL CONTEXT

I began this chapter by raising the question of the relation between science and politics in international affairs. In the subsequent discussion I described China's new international ties in science and technology and noted that these can be viewed as a rational attempt to overcome problems standing in the way of the four modernizations. In conclusion, however, it is useful to recall the place of these expanded ties in science and technology within the larger framework of Chinese foreign policy objectives. To illustrate this point, let us examine briefly China's relations with Japan.

Chinese scientific and technological relations with Europe are expanding and relations with the United States are at a new stage, but since the beginning of 1978 Japan seems to have occupied a special position in China's scientific and technological relations. This is most evident in commercial relations, but China and Japan are interested in increased scientific and educational cooperation as well. This was the conclusion of talks between Fang Yi and Seiji Kaya, a former president of Tokyo University, and between Education Minister Liu Xiyao and another former Tokyo University president, Ichiro Kato.[24]

These commercial and noncommercial contacts are resulting in large numbers of people moving between the two countries. Reportedly 10,000 Chinese technical experts visited Japan between 1973 and 1978.[25] Some 73 Chinese missions visited Japan in 1977, and by mid-1978 50 delegations had already gone. The number of Japanese visitors to China rose from 8,000 in 1972 to 30,000 in 1977.[26]

The Japanese, in short, seem to have an advantage over other capitalist countries not only in terms of trade, where the Japanese have long been preeminent, but also in what might be called "access." The greater access Japan has enjoyed in the past has in turn given Japan an advantage in selling technology to China and dominating the increasing number of technical consultancies. The latter in turn can increase access further.

The special relation between Japan and China is of course a product of geographical and cultural factors as well as of economic complementarity. But in addition, China approaches these relations at all three levels discussed above within a political framework. The ambitious goals of the four modernizations and the perception that international scientific and technological relations with Japan and other countries can contribute to meeting those goals have led to an alteration in the framework, but not its abandonment. Thus, contacts at the professional level—such as the number of Chinese sent abroad and their destinations—will be shaped by political considerations. The selection of foreign technology likewise has involved and will continue to involve judgments not only about the quality and appropriateness of the technology, but also about the extent to which a given transaction furthers Chinese foreign policy objectives. This is nicely illustrated by China's relations with Japan, which offer China a particularly fortuitous coincidence of interests. Not only does Japan offer China access to advanced science and technology, but China, by opening up its markets and by making available energy resources, believes it can achieve the major foreign policy objective of preventing closer Soviet-Japanese relations.

The new international dimensions of Chinese scientific and technological development strategy mark significant changes in Chinese policy and indicate a change in elite values and attitudes. Earlier in this report I noted the historic dimension of China's problematic relations with foreign science and material culture. The new policy should be viewed in the light of these historic considerations, which argue for caution in predicting full Chinese participation in international science and technology. However, they should also be seen in light of the opportunities international ties offer China in its attempts to manage domestic constraints on scientific and technological development. If present trends continue and participation expands, these international relations will have a significant influence on the kind of society China will be in the year 2000.

Chapter Six

◆◆◆

The Politics of Chinese Science and Sino-American Relations

I have suggested that international scientific and technological relations occur within a political framework resulting from the diplomatic interests and foreign policy objectives of the nations involved. International political interests in turn are linked to domestic politics. The interrelatedness of domestic and international affairs is particularly evident in Chinese science and technology today and in Sino-American scientific and technological relations.

China has established a new science policy and has embarked on a new road to scientific and technological development, which has included changes in the politics of science. Until the downfall of the Gang of Four, the politics of science were symbolic politics involving major cleavages over ideological views of science and the modes of scientific development. This clashing symbolism was integrally tied to struggles over power and positions within the network of organizations concerned with science and education. This pattern of conflict in turn was exacerbated by the imminence of China's first political succession.

The "old politics" has, at least for the time being, been put aside, and what appears to be a broad consensus on the mode of scientific development has emerged. Respect for, cultivation, and the rewarding of expertise in a stable, planned organizational environment are the features that characterize this mode of development. The new politics of science therefore will not immediately concern disputes over the mode of development, but instead will concern priorities for allocating resources within an accepted mode. Such disputes will occur over domestic research and development budgets, access to the means for procuring foreign technology, educational expenditures, and importantly, the allocation of technical manpower.

The Chinese political system can probably accommodate such disputes. The danger to Chinese scientific development in the short run is not that such disputes will lead to a return of the radical old politics of science, but that in attempting to accommodate allocative conflicts, the system will become more bureaucratized—overstaffed, excessively routinized, and therefore inflexible and intellectually flat. In short, the challenge of responding to the new politics of science is one of devising mechanisms for science policy and science administration that can achieve results by matching the potential advantages of socialist systems—the promises of planning and resource mobilization—with individual and group creativity.

The achievement of results, one suspects, is the key to avoiding a return to the more radical old politics of science. Although the prospect of such a change is remote at present, it is not totally absent. The present direction of policy represents a break with many values propagated actively during the past twelve years, values which large numbers of people embraced. The new policies clearly benefit some more than others. Among those disadvantaged, of particular interest are the members of the "lost generation," whose educations were upset by the Cultural Revolution and post–Cultural Revolution educational reforms. Members of this group are now entering their most active adult years with considerable experience in making revolution, but without the skills that the society now values. Although efforts are being made to accommodate the needs of this group, its members represent a potential core group for radical action if the investments in science and technology and the four modernizations generally do not pay off.

In terms of world history, the relation between political stability and scientific development is ambiguous and debatable. In modern China, however, the issue is less arguable. Recurrent political instability, from the mid-nineteenth century to the downfall of the Gang of Four, has been one of the major obstacles to scientific progress. The progress made in scientific development in the pre-1949 period is all the more remarkable because it was made in spite of periods of political chaos. Conversely, periods of stability since 1949 have been characterized by reasonable amounts of success in meeting the objectives of scientific development programs. The prospect for political stability in China for the remainder of the twentieth century is therefore fundamental in assessing the prospects for China's new scientific development programs. It is beyond the scope of this book to evaluate the prospect for political stability in general, but it is important to note the reciprocal relation between scientific development and political stability. Because of the high priority attached to science and technology as the keys to the four modernizations, the science system must demonstrate real achievements to justify the resources allocated to it. The main conditions for success, however, are continuing political stability and its concomitants of planned research and development activities, a stable organizational environment, and most important in the short run, uninterrupted educational programs.

China's new international posture on science and technology has as one of its two major purposes the use of resources available through international relations to overcome domestic constraints on development. In this sense China's new posture on international scientific and technological relations is intertwined with attempts to accommodate conflicting resource demands characteristic of the new politics of science. The quality of these relations, particularly the effectiveness of technology-transfer and foreign-training programs, can have a significant effect on China's scientific development and therefore on the new politics of science.

However, China's international posture has as another major purpose the development of mutual cooperation and understanding with other nations in order to counterbalance Soviet influence. This purpose can be discerned in China's relations with Japan. It can also be seen in relations with Western Europe and the United States. In short, in China's relations with Western Europe, the United States, and Japan, there are from the Chinese point of view overlapping interests. One one hand these relations offer access to the advanced science and technology required for the four modernizations. On the other hand, they offer opportunities to build relations with nations that continue to be uneasy about détente with the Soviet Union.

An entirely new era in Sino-American relations has begun as a result of the decision to normalize diplomatic relations. Cooperation in science and technology was a critical consideration in the deliberations leading to normalization, and it will undoubtedly continue to be a special feature of Sino-American relations. Indeed, future scientific and technological relations are likely to be an important factor influencing the quality of Sino-American political relations, and therefore these relations warrant continuing, detailed attention.

Since the Shanghai Communiqué of 1972, the focus of Sino-American scientific exchange has been the program administered by the Committee on Scholarly Communication with the People's Republic of China (CSCPRC)[1] on the U.S. side and by the Science and Technology Association on the Chinese side. By the end of 1978, there had been 37 Chinese delegations to the United States and 30 American delegations to China under this program.[2] These delegations had been useful to both sides as instruments for surveying the state of science in the two countries. However, both sides by 1978 wished to move beyond this mode of contact.

During July 1978, a major forward step in Sino-American scientific and technological relations was taken when President Carter's science advisor, Dr. Frank Press, led a delegation of high government science administrators to China. The delegation included representatives of most major federal science and technology agencies, including the National Aeronautics and Space Administration, the National Science Foundation, the National Institutes of Health, the Departments of Agriculture, Commerce, and Energy, and the U.S. Geological Survey.[3]

The Press mission was significant for several reasons. First, it led to the first official intergovernmental discussion of scientific cooperation involving the administrators of major science agencies. Second, it was an unusually high-level mission from the U.S. point of view, and it received a high-level reception in meetings with Vice-Premiers Deng Xiaoping and Fang Yi. Third, although both sides recognized the absence of normalized relations between the two countries as problematic, they agreed to an expansion of scientific and technological contacts in spite of the diplomatic relations issue. At the end of the visit, Press stated that he envisaged "a wide range of contact ... in the not too distant future, such as exchange of data, advanced seminars, cooperative research ventures, student exchanges, advanced training programs, and a growing commercial relationship in the civilian and technical sector."[4] And according to Fang Yi, if the normalization problem were removed, "vast vistas" would open up for the expansion of exchanges and cooperation,[5] which implied that although the immediate vistas were not vast, at least there were vistas.

The specific areas for cooperation discussed during the Press visit to Beijing included energy, public health, agriculture, oceanography, meteorology, natural resources exploration and development, and space. (Robert Frosch, an administrator of NASA, reportedly became the first foreigner to visit the Chinese satellite-assembly facilities.)[6]

The Press mission came at a time when U.S. relations with the Soviet Union were strained. The mission to China and the postponement of a scheduled visit by Press to Moscow, along with facilitated exports of sensitive technology to China[7] and restrictions on such exports to the USSR, were widely interpreted as part of a strategy of "playing the China card" against the Soviet Union. Indeed, when coupled with reports of unofficial advice to American scientists to cancel trips to the Soviet Union, from individuals at the State Department and National Academy of Sciences,[8] international scientific affairs were by the second half of 1978, an important, politicized component in the trilateral political relations involving the United States, China, and the Soviet Union. This fact added weight to the importance of the Press mission and to the expanding Sino-American scientific and technical relations.

As a result of the Press mission, it appeared that more substantive relations would begin even before formal diplomatic relations commenced. The development of contacts at the government-to-government level was the next logical step in the expansion of relations between the two countries.

Sino-American relations developed dramatically after the Press mission. In October 1978, a Sino-American understanding on the exchange of students and scholars was signed. In November and December, the fundamentals for a cooperation agreement in agriculture and energy were clarified during visits to China by Secretary of Agriculture Bergland and Secretary of Energy Schlesinger, and the foundations for cooperation in space were laid during a visit to the United States by a Chinese space delegation in November. Throughout this period, intensive discussions concerning political relations were also taking place. These discussions culminated in the December announcement that the two sides had reached agreement on the normalization of relations.

The decision on normalization was followed by the announcement that Deng Xiaoping would visit the United States in January 1979. During the visit of Deng's party, which significantly included Fang Yi, the preparations for further scientific and technological cooperation that had been made in 1978 were formalized by the signing of executive agreements by Vice-Premier Deng and President Carter, which among other things provided for a Joint Commission on Scientific and Technological Cooperation (see Appendix 1). Thus, a framework for greatly expanded scientific and technological relations at the professional, governmental, and commercial levels was established at the beginning of 1979, although difficult questions relating to controls over the export of sensitive technologies to China and the availability of Export-Import Bank credits remained to be solved. A further problem, the disposition of frozen assets, was solved expeditiously during Treasury Secretary Blumenthal's visit to China in March 1979.

From the U.S. point of view, expanded Sino-American scientific ties, apart from their inherent scientific value, are desirable for three reasons. First, they are a means of improving political relations with China in order to advance American interests at a time of a changing world balance of power. Second, they are a means of expanding mutually beneficial commercial relations. Finally, they offer opportunities to begin the process of building mutual understanding and cooperation with China on a range of increasingly important international issues of political economy involving science and technology.

American policy is based on the belief that American interests will be served by China's social and economic development and its emergence as a regional power. In addition, it is in the U.S. interest for China to develop its ability to produce food in order not to be a drain on world supplies and to produce energy in order to contribute to world supplies. Sino-American cooperation in science and technology will contribute to meeting these objectives.

As we have seen, the development of scientific and technological ties has gone hand in hand with the development of political relations. Although needlessly provocative talk of playing the China card was toned down as normalization approached, the United States has nevertheless made the point to the Soviet Union that it values its ties with China and appreciates China's efforts to become a strong, modern society. As of this writing, it seems fair to say that both the United States and China feel their security interests have been furthered by the closer ties that developed during 1978 and 1979. In addition, the new relationship offers the United States an opportunity to make contacts with China's next generation of technology-minded leaders.

Expanded scientific cooperation also has important implications for strengthened commercial relations. Because of the absence of diplomatic relations at the beginning of China's four modernizations program, the United States was at a disadvantage in commercial relations with China vis à vis Japan and Europe. Japan in particular has enjoyed a favored position in supplying China with needed technology, but the United States possesses a number of advantages, which for the most part could not be exploited prior to normalization.

Apart from purely technological advantages, owing to the competitiveness of U.S. industry in many areas of high technology desired by the Chinese, expanded contacts at the professional and governmental levels offer opportunities for wider commercial ties as well. U.S. leadership in many areas of basic science and government-organized big science and technology, particularly in China's eight priority areas for development, are advantages the United States has over other countries. The residue of good feeling toward the United States on the part of American-trained Chinese scientists is another factor in expanding U.S.-China relations, as are the many Chinese-American scientists and engineers with whom the Chinese feel comfortable.

In short, the Chinese have reasons to be enthusiastic about expanded contacts with the United States at the professional and governmental levels. Contacts at these two levels open up many opportunities for becoming more familiar with related commercial technology, hence they serve American commercial interests in the competition with Japan and, to a lesser extent, Europe in supplying China with advanced technology.

Of the eight high-priority areas for Chinese scientific and technological development, each—with the possible exception of high energy physics—has international political or economic significance as well as domestic importance. The successes and failures of Chinese research and development activities in agriculture and energy as noted above, as well as in materials, computers, space, lasers, and genetic engineering, will have policy ramifications for the international system and American interests. An obvious example is China's interest in developing nuclear fuel cycle technology and

U.S. interests in preventing the proliferation of sensitive nuclear technology. If the United States can expand its contacts with China, particularly at the professional and governmental levels, it will enjoy enhanced opportunities to work cooperatively with China in developing international policies in the interests of both countries. These opportunities are a third important reason why expanded U.S.-China scientific and technological relations are in the United States' interest.

American and Chinese officials have concluded that the case to be made for expanded scientific and technological relations is a good one, and the foundation for such relations has been laid. Nevertheless, as contacts expand, new problems will develop. Most of these cannot be readily anticipated, but successful policy planning requires, at the least, that attention be called to the adequacy of the process by which they might be solved. In examining process, both principles and mechanisms of action require attention. The more important principles (some of which are contained in the Science and Technology Agreement) are the following:

1. *Mutuality*: For the long-term viability of scientific and technological cooperation, some measure of mutuality must be incorporated into Sino-American relations. Because of the unequal levels of scientific development and material wealth, the achievement of mutuality in the short run will require special efforts.

   The principle of mutuality means that both parties give to the relationship and both parties receive benefits. The giving and taking need not occur on a narrowly conceived one-to-one basis, however. Rather, over the range of contacts and cooperative efforts, the costs and benefits to each side should average out. Thus, it is unlikely that direct mutuality can be achieved in cooperative research in the field of high energy physics, but it might be approached if the chemistry of natural products in the traditional Chinese pharmacopeia is considered as part of a package arrangement involving high energy physics. This idea of packaging areas of cooperation in the interest of mutuality implies that the organization for administering relations in the area of science be one with good relations with the full range of disciplinary subcommunities that constitute the American scientific community. In cooperation at the level of government agencies, the principle of mutuality should be interpreted to mean substantial cost sharing in cooperative efforts. The United States should not hesitate to inform the Chinese if it feels the principle of mutuality is not being met. The initial imbalance in student and scholar exchanges in China's favor is a case where the United States should vigorously assert the principle of mutuality.

2. *Open information*: To the extent that proprietary and national security considerations allow, expanded Sino-American cooperation should be

undertaken according to the principle of open information. Data and analyses resulting from cooperative efforts should be open to the scrutiny of the international scientific community.

3. *Noninterference*: As noted earlier, China's present level of interest and apparent willingness to participate in international science and technology mark some significant changes in policy. Such changes indicate a willingness to break with a pattern of attitudes about foreign culture that has historic roots as well as more immediate political and ideological antecedents. This policy change therefore involves risks on the Chinese side about the economic, political, and social consequences of expanded international contacts. For these reasons, the United States must be especially attentive to Chinese sensibilities that the increased access to Chinese society which closer scientific and technological relations will bring not be used to interfere in Chinese domestic affairs. Since the Chinese will be formally and informally seeking American advice and since the line between advice and interference is a thin one, observing the principle of noninterference may not be as easy as it appears.

4. *Gradualism*: Some of the considerations underlying the principle of noninterference pertain to the principle of gradualism as well. The Chinese cannot be rushed into expanded cooperation, and the United States should not be tempted to seek relations with short-term symbolic value without the promise of longer-term relations of substance. The United States should also be wary of Chinese attempts to promote projects of symbolic value for political purposes or of one-sided value to China. The principle of mutuality can serve as a guide to the interpretation of the principle of gradualism. New joint projects, agreements, and cooperative endeavors should be implemented only when both sides understand clearly how their interests will be served and what the costs will be.

The principle of gradualism is particularly important in the early stages of expanded relations. China's intentions for expanded foreign contacts and the views of Chinese leaders on the scope and limits of such contacts are still not clear. Furthermore, the differences between the two societies are great, and the years of mutual isolation and suspicion have resulted in enormous mutual ignorance. To approach China with facile assumptions about what is and is not possible in the way of expanded scientific and technological contacts is to invite disappointment and misunderstanding. The principle of gradualism is intended to insure that friendship and cooperation are built on a solid foundation.

5. *Nth Country Awareness*: Bilateral Sino-American scientific and tech-

nological relations will not develop in a vacuum. As we have seen, China has considerable interest in scientific relations with other countries, as does the United States. The principle of nth country awareness calls for the development of Sino-American relations based on an awareness of implications for other countries. It may seem trivial to urge nth country awareness since presumably this is a normal part of foreign policymaking. However, it is often neglected in the event. The bureaucratic structures that shape foreign policy are after all imperfect, and assumed mechanisms for communication and coordination often fail.

The principle of nth country awareness is intended to insure that the development of Sino-American scientific relations does not inadvertently disturb relations with countries, such as Japan, with whom both China and the United States have separate bilateral interests and potential trilateral or multilateral interests.

The United States should in its dealings with China consider the implications for regional relations, particularly in the Pacific Basin. There are indications of a movement toward greater Pacific Basin regional integration, and the United States should consider its relations with China in that context and its relations with the Pacific Basin in the context of relations with China. Some of the prospective areas for scientific and technological cooperation, such as energy research, have implications for multilateral cooperative relations, as we have seen. The United States should consider these implications in its dealings with China and in particular should clarify the implications of U.S. encouragement of Chinese participation in multilateral arrangements.

Within a framework of principles such as these, initiatives for continuing expansion of cooperation can be made. However, in order to turn initiatives into opportunities and to avoid opportunities becoming serious mistakes, the United States must give more consideration to the organization and administration of Sino-American scientific and technological relations. Three questions in particular warrant attention. The first concerns the organization of the new embassy in Beijing. Are the interests of scientific and technological relations adequately represented in the embassy? Is the representation commensurate with the importance attached to those relations? An embassy office for scientific and noncommercial technological affairs should have the responsibility for collecting and maintaining information on Chinese science and of matching that information with opportunities for cooperation within the framework of American foreign policy. It is important that such an office be staffed by persons who are familiar with the domestic and international workings of American federal agencies, who understand the social and political settings of Chinese scientific activities, and who are familiar with academic science in the United States. Indeed, it may be desirable for this office to employ an American university scientist recruited to government service in Beijing for two or three years.

Effective administration and further development of Sino-American scientific relations also require an organization for administering these relations in Washington. Here the operative questions are: Do Sino-American relations in science and technology receive the priority attention they deserve? Is there a center of responsibility for the management of these relations? And does this center have both the influence to achieve interagency coordination and the ability to develop sufficient China expertise? One might also ask whether the organizational arrangements chosen reflect the fact that an overview of the activities at the three levels of interaction discussed in the previous chapter is required.

At the intergovernmental level, the lead organization in orchestrating expanded scientific relations has been the Office of Science and Technology Policy (OSTP). The OSTP is to act as the executive agent of the United States for the Joint Commission on Scientific and Technological Cooperation. The useful role OSTP has played is closely related to the personal interests in U.S.-China relations shown by Frank Press acting within a framework of presidential commitment to improved ties with China. A different president with a different science adviser may have other priorities.

Dramatic events, such as the normalization of relations and the visit of Deng Xiaoping, have the effect of bringing issues and problems to the attention of high-level government centers of policy and coordination, such as the OSTP. However, once high-level political decisions and political rituals successfully create a framework for further cooperation and the drama passes, responsibility for the conduct of scientific and technological relations devolves to specialized, mission-oriented agencies. Since these agencies have the expertise required for and concrete interests in cooperative activities, this devolution is only right and proper. A possible cost, however, is the emergence of problems involving interagency coordination in the interest of advancing foreign policy goals. The danger of this potential problem becoming an actual problem would be lessened if an effective mechanism for such coordination existed.

The OSTP working in conjunction with the Federal Coordinating Council for Science, Engineering, and Technology would appear to be an appropriate candidate for future interagency coordination and policy development. However, the OSTP is seriously understaffed and must deal with a variety of domestic and international science policy questions that have nothing to do with China, and the role of the FCCSET in international affairs has not been notable. In the press of other problems, the special concern shown for relations with China in late 1978 and early 1979 is likely to be lost.

Of course it is unreasonable to expect that the same degree of special attention to China shown in this period will continue. It might be argued that as a result of the breakthrough on normalization, the United States should allow patterns of routinization to develop and that responsibility for overseeing the policy aspects of U.S.-China scientific relations should be assumed by the State Department, where it rightfully belongs. Unfortunately, however, the State Department has long had difficulties in developing and maintaining the capabilities to deal with international scientific and technological affairs and to counterbalance the propensities of mission-oriented agencies toward relatively independent action in their conduct of international programs. Current efforts to strengthen the State Department's role hold promise, but for the moment effective interagency policy development and control are more a matter of the interests of and relations among certain key officials than an institutionalized process.

A more fundamental question is: Do scientific relations with China warrant special administrative arrangements to avoid premature routinization? The answer to the question depends in part on the degree of importance attached to China in American foreign policy. On the assumption that close relations with China have now become an objective of major importance in American foreign policy and on the basis of the special problems of Chinese science policy and scientific development described in the preceding chapters, one can infer that to allow scientific relations with China to be routinized prematurely and devolve to more decentralized bureaucratic processes would be a serious mistake. It remains to be seen whether the establishment of the Joint Commission on Scientific and Technological Cooperation will contribute to the avoidance of this problem.

The third of our three questions concerning the adequacy of organizational arrangements for the management of Sino-American scientific ties can be restated as follows: Does the United States have, either inside or outside government, policy-analysis capabilities relevant to the administration of scientific relations with China? This question stems from the belief that effective development of Sino-American scientific and technological relations over the long run will require sustained attention to and reflective analysis of developments both in Chinese science and science policy and in the actual conduct of the relations.

Unfortunately, neither the government nor American universities now has this capability. The analytic tasks involved are appropriate to the university community. However, attention to questions about the role of science and technology in Chinese modernization and in Chinese foreign relations has been negligible at the China studies centers of major universities. Furthermore, university centers for the study of science, technology, and public policy are notable for their near total lack of competence in Chinese affairs. It would therefore be a service to the cause of Sino-American relations for the government—perhaps appropriately the OSTP—to take the initiative in establishing one or more centers for the study of Chinese scientific affairs to serve as the focal point for American scholarship on this critical aspect of Chinese modernization.

The discussion above is not based on the assumption that scientific and technological relations are a substitute for political relations. Rather, it is offered in the belief that at certain times and under certain conditions, scientific and technological relations play a significant role in improving political relations and in achieving foreign policy objectives. The period since the middle of 1977 has been such a time. It has been and continues to be a time of unusual confluence of Chinese and American foreign policy objectives, of an unprecedented domestic political commitment in China to scientific development, and of American preeminence in many fields of science and technology. The conjunction of these factors creates a unique opportunity for expanding scientific and technological relations, which, if conducted properly, can greatly enhance Sino-American friendship and understanding.

At best, the preceding pages can be understood as an interim report on science and technology in China's drive for modernization. Since China's commitment to the four modernizations began again in earnest in 1977, there have been a number of adjustments in this ambitious program. Doubtless, there will be more.

In this study, I have attempted to describe and set in historical perspective what I take to be China's ongoing, long-term objectives. I then addressed questions concerning the major constraints on scientific and technological developments. International scientific and technological relations were seen as offering China additional options in its attempts to manage those constraints. United States policy toward China has appropriately taken this fact into consideration.

However, I have suggested that Chinese foreign scientific and technological relations also involve important foreign policy objectives of a political nature. In addition, they are complicated by the historically and ideologically problematic reaction China has shown to foreign knowledge and material culture. The choices facing U.S. policymakers therefore are considerably more complex than they would be if the issue were only one of rendering China scientific or technological assistance.

The implications of China's drive for scientific and technological modernization for U.S. policy could not be fully discussed in this study. To do so would have required a more thorough analysis of U.S. and Chinese interests and foreign policy objectives than my topic allowed. Instead, I have assumed that the improvement of relations with China is an important objective of U.S. policy, and that scientific and technological ties will continue to contribute importantly to political relations, as they have in the immediate past. Given these assumptions and the complex of considerations involved in China's new interest in international scientific and technological affairs, I have argued that U.S. attention to the principles and administrative structures involved in the conduct of scientific and technological relations must be commensurate with the importance attached to China in American foreign policy.

The importance of the conduct of relations cannot be overstressed. The past century of Sino-American relations have been characterized by extremes of friendship and hostility, but not by a great deal of mutual understanding and respect. The achievement of mutual understanding and respect takes time and patience, which in turn requires attention to process. We now know enough about the conduct of foreign affairs to recognize that attention to process means attention to the structures and interactions of organizations and the realism of the principles by which they operate. In this chapter, I have attempted to focus attention on process—on organization and principles of conducting relations—in the belief that these questions are too often ignored. Given the context of Chinese scientific development, inattention to process can undermine the foundations of what now promises to become a new era in Sino-American relations.

Appendix One

◆━━◆━━◆

Agreements Between the Governments of the United States and the People's Republic of China on Cooperation in Science and Technology

A. AGREEMENT BETWEEN
THE GOVERNMENT OF THE UNITED STATES OF AMERICA
AND THE GOVERNMENT OF THE PEOPLE'S REPUBLIC OF CHINA
ON COOPERATION IN SCIENCE AND TECHNOLOGY

The Government of the United States of America and the Government of the People's Republic of China (hereinafter referred to as the Contracting Parties);

Acting in the spirit of the Joint Communiqué on the Establishment of Diplomatic Relations between the United States of America and the People's Republic of China;

Recognizing that cooperation in the fields of science and technology can promote the well-being and prosperity of both countries;

Affirming that such cooperation can strengthen friendly relations between both countries;

Wishing to establish closer and more regular cooperation between scientific and technical entities and personnel in both countries;

Have agreed as follows:

ARTICLE 1

1. The Contracting Parties shall develop cooperation under this agreement on the basis of equality, reciprocity and mutual benefit.

2. The principal objective of this Agreement is to provide broad opportunities for cooperation in scientific and technological fields of mutual interest, thereby promoting the progress of science and technology for the benefit of both countries and of mankind.

ARTICLE 2

Cooperation under this Agreement may be undertaken in the fields of agriculture, energy, space, health, environment, earth sciences, engineering, and such other areas of science and technology and their management as may be mutually agreed, as well as educational and scholarly exchange.

ARTICLE 3

Cooperation under this Agreement may include:

a. Exchange of scientists, scholars, specialists and students;

b. Exchange of scientific, scholarly, and technological information and documentation;

c. Joint planning and implementation of programs and projects;

d. Joint research, development and testing, and exchange of research results and experience between cooperating entities;

e. Organization of joint courses, conferences and symposia;

f. Other forms of scientific and technological cooperation as may be mutually agreed.

ARTICLE 4

Pursuant to the objectives of this Agreement, the Contracting Parties shall encourage and facilitate, as appropriate, the development of contacts and cooperation between government agencies, universities, organizations, institutions, and other entities of both countries, and the conclusion of accords between such bodies for the conduct of cooperative activities. Both sides will further promote, consistent with such cooperation and where appropriate, mutually beneficial bilateral economic activities.

ARTICLE 5

Specific accords implementing this Agreement may cover the subjects of cooperation, procedures to be followed, treatment of intellectual property, funding and other appropriate matters. With respect to funding, costs shall be borne as mutually agreed. All cooperative activities under this Agreement shall be subject to the availability of funds.

ARTICLE 6

Cooperative activities under this Agreement shall be subject to the laws and regulations in each country.

ARTICLE 7

Each Contracting Party shall, with respect to cooperative activities under this Agreement, use its best efforts to facilitate prompt entry into and exit from its territory of equipment and personnel of the other side, and also to provide access to relevant geographic areas, institutions, data and materials.

ARTICLE 8

Scientific and technological information derived from cooperative activities under this Agreement may be made available, unless otherwise agreed in an implementing accord under Article 5, to the world scientific community through customary channels and in accordance with the normal procedures of the participating entities.

ARTICLE 9

Scientists, technical experts, and entities of third countries or international organizations may be invited, upon mutual consent of both sides, to participate in projects and programs being carried out under this Agreement.

ARTICLE 10

1. The Contracting Parties shall establish a US-PRC Joint Commission on Scientific and Technological Cooperation, which shall consist of United States and Chinese parts. Each Contracting Party shall designate a co-chairman and its members of the Commission. The Commission shall adopt procedures for its operation, and shall ordinarily meet once a year in the United States and the People's Republic of China alternately.

2. The Joint Commission shall plan and coordinate cooperation in science and technology, and monitor and facilitate such cooperation. The Commission shall also consider proposals for the further development of cooperative activities in specific areas and recommend measures and programs to both sides.

3. To carry out its functions, the Commission may when necessary create temporary or permanent joint subcommittees or working groups.

4. During the period between meetings of the Commission, additions or amendments may be made to already approved cooperative activities, as may be mutually agreed.

5. To assist the Joint Commission, each Contracting Party shall designate an Executive Agent. The Executive Agent on the United States side shall be the Office of Science and Technology Policy; and on the side of the People's Republic of China, the State Scientific and Technological Commission. The Executive Agents shall collaborate closely to promote proper implementation of all activities and programs. The Executive Agent of each Contracting Party shall be responsible for coordinating the implementation of its side of such activities and programs.

ARTICLE 11

1. This Agreement shall enter into force upon signature and shall remain in force for five years. It may be modified or extended by mutual agreement of the Parties.

2. The termination of this Agreement shall not affect the validity or duration of any implementing accords made under it.

B. *TEXT OF LETTER TO FANG YI*

His Excellency
Fang Yi
Minister in Charge
The State Scientific and
    Technological Commission
Beijing

Dear Mr. Minister:

With reference to the Agreement Between the United States of America and the People's Republic of China on Cooperation in Science and Technology, signed in Washington today, it is the understanding of the Government of the United States of America that existing understandings in the fields of education, agriculture and space will become a part of the formal specific accords to be concluded in those fields under Article 5 of the Agreement.

Attached as annexes to this letter are the Understanding on the Exchange of Students and Scholars reached in Washington in October 1978, the Understanding on Agricultural Exchange reached in Beijing in November 1978, and the Understanding on Cooperation in Space Technology reached in Washington in December 1978.

If the Government of the People's Republic of China confirms this understanding and the texts of the understandings annexed hereto, this letter and the letter of confirmation of the People's Republic of China will constitute an agreement relating to these fields between our two governments.

Sincerely,
DIRECTOR
Office of Science
and Technology Policy

C. *UNDERSTANDING ON THE EXCHANGE OF STUDENTS AND SCHOLARS BETWEEN THE UNITED STATES OF AMERICA AND THE PEOPLE'S REPUBLIC OF CHINA*

An understanding on educational exchanges between the United States and China was reached in Washington, D.C. in October 1978 during discussions between the Chinese education delegation headed by Dr. Zhou Peiyuan, Acting Chairman of the

PRC Science and Technology Association, and the U.S. education delegation headed by Dr. Richard C. Atkinson, Director of the National Science Foundation, as follows:

1. Both sides agreed they would pursue a program of educational exchange in accordance with and in implementation of the spirit of the Shanghai Communiqué;

2. There will be a two-way scientific and scholarly exchange which will provide mutual benefit to both countries;

3. The exchanges will include students, graduate students and visiting scholars for programs of research and study in each country;

4. The two sides exchanged lists of fields in which its students and scholars are interested and lists of institutions where they wish to work. Each side will use its best efforts to fulfill the requests of the other for study and research opportunities. Each side will expeditiously grant visas for such exchanges in accordance with its laws and regulations,

5. The sending side will pay the costs associated with its participants;

6. Both sides may take full advantage of any scholarships which may be offered;

7. Each side will be responsible for the implementation of the program in its territory, including responsibility for providing advice to the other side and relevant information and materials about the universities and research institutions concerned;

8. The two sides agreed that the students and scholars sent by both sides should observe the laws and regulations and respect the customs of the receiving country;

9. The Chinese side indicated it wishes to send a total of 500 to 700 students and scholars in the academic year 1978–1979. The United States side indicated it wishes to send 10 students in its national program in January 1979 and 50 students in its national program by September 1979 as well as such other numbers as the Chinese side is able to receive. Both sides agreed to use their best efforts to implement such programs;

10. To set each year the number of students and scholars to be exchanged and to discuss the progress of the program of exchanges, the two sides will meet when necessary. Consultations on important matters may also be held by the governments of the two countries. In addition, both sides will encourage direct contacts between the universities, research institutions, and scholars of their respective countries;

11. Both sides believe that the discussions mark a good beginning and have opened up the prospect of broadened opportunities for exchanges between the two countries in the fields of science, technology and education as relations between them improve. Both sides also believe that such exchanges are conducive to the promotion of friendship and understanding between their two peoples.

D. UNDERSTANDING ON AGRICULTURAL EXCHANGE BETWEEN THE UNITED STATES OF AMERICA AND THE PEOPLE'S REPUBLIC OF CHINA

During a visit to China of a delegation led by U.S. Secretary of Agriculture Robert Bergland in November 1978, discussions were held with Chinese officials which resulted in understandings concerning US-PRC agricultural exchange. It was agreed that it would be of mutual benefit to promote cooperation in agricultural technology, economic information, science and education, and trade in agricultural products, and that contacts between organizations and institutions of all types in these fields should be facilitated.

It was noted that study groups had already been exchanged in the fields of science and research, farm machinery, citrus fruits, wheat and vegetables. It was agreed that areas in which further exchanges should occur would include germ plasm (seed research and selection), biological control of pests, livestock and veterinary science, and agricultural education and research management methods. It was also agreed that, within the next two or three years, cooperation would be carried out in the fields of forestry, agricultural engineering, improvement of grasslands and management of pasturelands, cultivation of fruit trees, medicinal plants, and the application of remote sensing and computer technology to agriculture. Such cooperation would include mutual visits of, and joint research by, students, scientists and technicians.

The U.S. side agreed to facilitate contacts between officials of the People's Republic of China and U.S. manufacturers of agricultural equipment and supplies. Each side expressed its interest in the statistical methods of agricultural economics and experience in agricultural management of the other side. It was agreed also that, through the cooperator program of the U.S. Department of Agriculture, further discussions should be held regarding the products and technology best suited to conditions in China and that USDA teams would begin visiting China in early 1979. Reciprocal scientific teams from the PRC will also begin U.S. study visits in 1979.

It was agreed that the development of agricultural trade between the two countries was in the mutual interest and that its prospects were bright.

It was agreed that when study teams or technical trainees are exchanged on a one-for-one basis, the host country would pay in-country costs; and that when the exchange is not reciprocal, the sending country will pay all costs.

E. UNDERSTANDING ON COOPERATION IN SPACE TECHNOLOGY
BETWEEN THE UNITED STATES OF AMERICA AND
THE PEOPLE'S REPUBLIC OF CHINA

During a visit to the United States in November and December 1978 by a delegation headed by Dr. Ren Xinmin, Director of the Chinese Academy of Space Technology, an understanding in principle was reached with a delegation headed by Dr. Robert A. Frosch, Administrator of the National Aeronautics and Space Administration, on U.S.-Chinese cooperation in the peaceful utilization of space technology.

This understanding includes:

1. Cooperation in the development of the civil broadcasting and communications system of the PRC. The PRC intends, under suitable conditions, to purchase a U.S. satellite broadcasting and communications system, including the associated ground receiving and distribution equipment. The space portion of the system will be

launched by NASA and placed in geostationary orbit by a U.S. contractor, with continued operation to be carried out by China; and

2. The intended purchase, under suitable conditions, by the PRC of a U.S. ground station capable of receiving earth resources information from the NASA Landsat remote sensing satellites, including the Landsat now under development.

It was also agreed that, through further discussions and correspondence, both sides would develop the details of the understanding described above and consider other fields of civil space cooperation which could be of mutual interest and benefit.

F. IMPLEMENTING ACCORD BETWEEN THE DEPARTMENT OF ENERGY OF THE UNITED STATES OF AMERICA AND THE STATE SCIENTIFIC AND TECHNOLOGICAL COMMISSION OF THE PEOPLE'S REPUBLIC OF CHINA ON COOPERATION IN THE FIELD OF HIGH ENERGY PHYSICS

The Department of Energy of the United States of America and the State Scientific and Technological Commission of the People's Republic of China (hereinafter referred to as the Parties), for the purpose of promoting cooperation and collaboration in the field of high energy physics subject to the Agreement Between the Government of the United States of America and the Government of the People's Republic of China on Cooperation in Science and Technology, signed in Washington, D.C. on January 31, 1979, have agreed as follows:

ARTICLE 1

The objective of this Accord is to further the energy programs of the Parties by establishing a framework for cooperation in the field of high energy physics, including theoretical and experimental research, accelerator design and construction techniques; and related technology areas as may be mutually agreed.

ARTICLE 2

Cooperation under this Accord may include the following forms:

1. Exchange and provision of information on scientific and technical developments, activities, and practices;

2. Research and development activities in the form of experiments, tests, and other technical collaborative activities;

3. Exchange of scientists, engineers, and other specialists; including visits by specialist teams or individuals to the facilities of the other Party, and exchange of personnel for training purposes;

4. Exchange and provision of samples, materials, instruments, and components for testing and evaluation;

5. Such other forms of cooperation as are mutually agreed.

ARTICLE 3

Specific undertakings, obligations and conditions with respect to the conduct of each activity under Article 2 including responsibility for payment of costs shall be agreed by authorized entities on a case-by-case basis.

ARTICLE 4

1. For the purpose of coordinating activities pursuant to this Accord, a Committee on High Energy Physics is hereby established, consisting of representatives of the Parties and such other persons from each Party's national research community as it may designate. Each Party shall designate one person to act as its co-chairperson on the Committee.

2. The Committee will encourage contacts between scientists, universities, and laboratories of the two nations.

3. The Committee each year shall develop and maintain a listing of joint activities to be carried out, and, as requested by the participating institutions and scientists, shall assist with arrangements for the listed activities. Items may be listed by consensus at meetings of the Committee, or, between meetings, by agreement of the co-chairpersons.

4. Each Party shall designate its members of the Committee within two months of the effective date of this Accord. The first meeting of the Committee should be held, if possible, within three months thereafter at an agreed site. Subsequently, the Committee shall meet in the United States and the People's Republic of China alternately at intervals of about 12 months or as agreed by the co-chairpersons.

5. The Committee shall be subject to the direction of the US-PRC Joint Commission on Scientific and Technological Cooperation established under the aforesaid Agreement of January 31, 1979, and shall periodically report the Status of its program to that Commission.

6. The Committee may assume other duties as mutually agreed by the Parties.

ARTICLE 5

The application or use of any information exchanged or transferred between the Parties under this Accord shall be the responsibility of the Party receiving it, and the transmitting Party does not warrant the suitability of such information for any particular use or application.

ARTICLE 6

The Parties recognize the need to agree upon provisions concerning protection of copyrights and treatment of inventions or discoveries made or conceived in the course of or under this Accord in order to facilitate specific activities hereunder. Accordingly, the Parties shall appoint experts in these two fields who shall separately recommend to the Parties detailed provisions which, if the Parties agree, shall be made an Annex to this Accord.

ARTICLE 7

Both Parties agree that in the event equipment is to be exchanged, or supplied by one Party to the other for use in cooperative activities, they shall enter into specific understandings on a case-by-case basis.

ARTICLE 8

1. Whenever an attachment of staff is contemplated under this Accord each Party shall ensure that staff with necessary skills and competence are selected for attachment to the other Party.

2. Each attachment of staff shall be the subject of an exchange of letters between the participating institutions, covering funding and other matters of interest not otherwise specified in this Accord.

3. Each Party shall provide all necessary assistance to the attached staff (and their families) of the other Party as regards administrative formalities, travel arrangements and accommodations.

4. The staff of each Party shall conform to the general rules of work and safety regulations in force at the host establishment, or as agreed in separate attachment of staff agreements.

ARTICLE 9

1. All questions related to this Accord or activities carried out hereunder shall be settled by mutual agreement of the Parties.

2. Each Party will accept liability to the extent authorized by its national laws for damages arising from cooperative activities under this Accord.

ARTICLE 10

1. This accord shall enter into force upon signature, and, unless terminated earlier in accordance with paragraph 2 of this Article, shall remain in force for a five-year period. It may be amended or extended by mutual agreement of the Parties.

2. This Accord may be terminated at any time at the discretion of either Party, upon 6 months advance notification in writing by the Party seeking to terminate the Accord.

3. The termination of this Accord shall not affect the validity or duration of specific activities being undertaken hereunder.

Appendix Two

◆◆◆

China's New Invention Law

*REGULATIONS OR REWARDS FOR INVENTIONS IN THE
PEOPLE'S REPUBLIC OF CHINA:*

ARTICLE I

These regulations are specially formulated to encourage inventions, promote modernizations of science and technology and accelerate socialist construction.

ARTICLE II

The inventions mentioned in these regulations refer to major new scientific and technological achievements which must also meet the following three conditions:

1. Never achieved before;
2. Advanced;
3. Proved applicable through practice.

ARTICLE III

The State Scientific and Technological Commission of the People's Republic of China (hereafter referred to as the State Scientific Commission) exercises unified leadership over the work of rewarding inventions throughout the whole country. The various departments of the State Council and the provincial, municipal and autonomous regional scientific and technological commissions (hereafter referred to as provincial, municipal and autonomous regional scientific commissions) are responsible for leading the work in reporting and examining inventions in each department and locality.

SOURCE: NCNA.

ARTICLE IV

Inventors' (collective or individual) reports on inventions should include the following details:
1. Name of invention;
2. Detailed description of invention;
3. Name of inventor;
4. Justification for regard as an invention;
5. Time invention was finished;
6. Date of report;
7. Reporting unit and comments on examination;

ARTICLE V

Procedures for reporting and handling of inventions are as follows:

1. Inventions are reported by inventors through the chain of command in organizations they belong to. At the same time copies of the reports are sent to provincial, municipal or autonomous regional scientific commissions and responsible departments of the State Council.

2. Upon receipt of reports on inventions, provincial, municipal or autonomous regional departments and bureaus should promptly conduct examinations, and those meeting the provisions of Article II should be reported to the relevant provincial, municipal or autonomous regional scientific commissions and responsible departments of the State Council.

3. Scientific and technological associations and academic societies at various levels under a province, municipality or autonomous region can make recommendations on inventions to relevant departments and bureaus of that province, municipality or autonomous region; The China Scientific and Technical Association and the various academic societies can recommend items of inventions to responsible departments of the State Council.

4. The provincial, municipal or autonomous regional scientific commissions and the responsible departments of the State Council should promptly organize examinations of the inventions reported, and those meeting the provisions in Article II should be graded for rewards and reported on the State Scientific Commission.

5. The State Scientific Commission will set up an evaluation committee for inventions to be responsible for evaluating inventions and grading them for reward. Rewards will be conferred after approval by the State Scientific Commission.

6. The procedures for reporting and screening inventions for specific national defense purposes will be laid out separately by the National Defense Scientific and Technological Commission (hereafter referred to as the National Defense Scientific Commission); and the National Defense Industry Office. Inventions for specific national defense purposes which have been examined, graded for rewards and approved by the National Defense Scientific Commission or the National Defense

Industry Office will be reported to the State Scientific Commission for approval, and rewards will then be given.

ARTICLE VI

In rewarding inventions, it is necessary to adhere to the principle of putting proletarian politics in command and combining spiritual encouragement and material rewards with the emphasis on spiritual encouragement.

Rewards for inventions are divided into four categories according to their importance. The rewards, including honors rewards and cash rewards, are as follows:

1. An invention certificate, a medal and 10,000 yuan.
2. An invention certificate, a medal and 5,000 yuan.
3. An invention certificate, a medal and 2,000 yuan.
4. An invention certificate, a medal and 1,000 yuan.

ARTICLE VII

Inventions of extraordinary importance shall be given special grade rewards, which should be reported by the State Scientific Commission to the State Council for approval.

ARTICLE VIII

Cash rewards for inventions by collectives (including coordinated units) should be reasonably divided among members according to their respective contributions. Cash rewards for inventions by individuals should be issued to those individuals.

ARTICLE IX

All inventions belong to the state. All units throughout the country (including units enforcing the system of collective ownership) may make use of inventions as needed.

ARTICLE X

Responsible departments under the State Council should offer suggestions on the publication of the particulars of an invention and on its classification, which should be reported to the State Scientific Commission for approval. The publication of the particulars of an invention for special use in national defense and its classification should be approved by the Science and Technology Commission for National Defense or by the Defense Industry Office.

ARTICLE XI

Before the particulars of classified inventions are supplied to foreign countries for foreign trade or other reasons, they must be approved by the State Scientific Commission.

ARTICLE XII

Overseas Chinese residing in foreign countries and foreigners may report their inventions to the State Scientific Commission. They will be examined and approved for rewards according to this regulation.

ARTICLE XIII

Controversies over inventions may be reported to higher-level organs which should seriously investigate, examine and handle such controversies.

ARTICLE XIV

All departments and units should encourage the masses to provide inventions and take a serious, scientific approach of seeking truth from facts. While enforcing the reward system, they must step up their ideological and political work, promote the socialist spirit of coordination and oppose such unhealthy trends as departmental egoism, individualism and lack of coordination. Those who hit at or suppress others trying to make inventions and who resort to deception regarding inventions or steal others' fruits of labor should be criticized, educated and rectified. Those involved in serious cases should be dealt with sternly or punished according to law.

ARTICLE XV

This regulation becomes effective the day the State Council makes it public. (December 28, 1978).

Notes

1: THE ROOTS OF A NEW SCIENCE POLICY

1. " 'Abridgement' of Fang Yi Report to National Science Conference," New China News Agency (NCNA) dispatch, March 28, 1978, in *Foreign Broadcast Information Service (FBIS)*, March 29, 1978.
2. *Peking Review* 1978, no. 23 (June 9): 3–4.
3. Chinese Academy of Sciences (CAS), Institute of Mathematics, Mass Criticism Group, "The Party's Policy Toward the Intellectuals Brooks No Tampering," *Guangming ribao (GMRB)*, September 3, 1976, in U.S. Consulate General, Hong Kong, *Survey of the People's Republic of China Press (SPRCP)* 6206.
4. Fang Yi, "On the Situation In China's Science and Education," *Peking Review* 1978, no. 2 (January 13): 15–17.
5. Leo A. Orleans, "Scientific and Technical Manpower," in Organization for Economic Cooperation and Development, ed., *Science and Technology in the People's Republic of China* (Paris: OECD, 1977), p. 19.
6. These observations are based upon reflections contained in a number of trip reports written by American scientific delegations to China. See in particular, Committee on Scholarly Communications with the People's Republic of China, ed., *Solid State Physics in the People's Republic of China* (Washington, D.C.: National Academy of Sciences, 1976).
7. Fang Yi, "Science and Education," p. 18.
8. Hua Guofeng, "Unite and Strive to Build a Modern, Powerful Socialist Country," *Peking Review* 1978, no. 10 (March 10): 18–31. Western observers and the Chinese themselves do not regard Hua's remarks as an operational plan containing immediately realizable goals. I believe it is a fair statement of aspirations, however, and it is treated as such in this study.
9. Hu Yaobang was named party secretary general in January 1979. This post was last occupied by Deng Xiaoping before the Cultural Revolution. Hu Qiaomu has become the president of the new Academy of Social Sciences. Both men were longtime associates of Deng.
10. This analysis is drawn from Ministry of Education, Mass Criticism Group, "A Political Struggle Around the Question of the Basic Theories of Natural Science," *GMRB* January 16, 1977, in *SPRCP* 77-4; and Zhou Peiyuan, "What Is the Intention of the Gang of Four in Obstructing Research on Basic Theories?" *Renmin ribao (RMRB)*, January 13, 1977, in *SPRCP* 77-4.
11. Ministry of Education, Mass Criticism Group, "Political Struggle."

12. Ibid.

13. Zhou Peiyuan, "The Intention of the Gang of Four"; *China News Analysis* 1070 (February 18, 1977).

14. Ministry of Education, Mass Criticism Group, "Political Struggle."

15. Ibid.; CAS, Theoretical Group, "A Shocking Struggle Which Occurred In the Science and Technology Circles," *RMRB*, March 9, 1977.

16. CAS, Theoretical Group, "Shocking Struggle"; Ministry of Education, Mass Criticism Group, "Political Struggle."

17. CAS, Theoretical Group, "Shocking Struggle."

18. NCNA dispatch, July 7, 1977, in *FBIS*, July 11, 1977; *RMRB*, July 6, 1977, in *FBIS*, July 11, 1977; Changchun provincial service, September 28, 1977, in *FBIS*, October 5, 1977.

2: ORGANIZATION AND PLANNING

1. Fang Yi, "On the Situation in China's Science and Education," *Peking Reivew* 1978, no. 2 (January 13): 16–17.

2. Ibid., p. 16.

3. According to one version of the "Outline Report," the STC and the CAS were merged in 1970. See *Ming Pao* (Hong Kong), July 5, 1977.

4. For an excellent summary of these activities, see Thomas Fingar and Genevieve Dean, *Developments in PRC Science and Technology Policy, October-December, 1977,* S & T Summary no. 5 (Stanford: Stanford University, United States–China Relations Program, n.d.).

5. This general subject is discussed in Richard P. Suttmeier, "Chinese Scientific Societies and Chinese Scientific Development," *Developing Economies* 11, no. 2 (Autumn, 1973): 146–63.

6. Zhou Peiyuan, "Launching the Drive to Modernize Science," *China Reconstructs*, July 1978, p. 5.

7. The first class admitted to institutions of higher education after the new entrance examinations went into effect numbered 278,000. In October 1978, a second class, numbering 290,000, was admitted. (*Beijing Review* 1979, no. 3 [January 19]: 31.) Reportedly 9,000 students were to be enrolled in graduate programs by autumn, 1978. It is expected that some 10,000 individuals will have begun overseas study by 1985. (Pierre M. Perrolle, "Engineering Education in China: A Report on Observations of the U.S. Engineering Education Delegation to China, September 8–October 2, 1978" [Paper delivered at the Workshop on the Development of Industrial Science and Technology in the PRC: Implications for U.S. Policy, St. George, Bermuda, January 3–7, 1979].)

8. Fang Yi, "Science and Education," p. 18.

9. The areas singled out were atomic energy, electronics, jet propulsion, automation, petroleum and scarce mineral exploration, metallurgy, fuel technology, power equipment and heavy machinery, Yellow and Yangtze River development, chemical fertilizer and agricultural mechanization, prevention and eradication of detrimental diseases, and basic theory.

10. See Richard P. Suttmeier, *Research and Revolution* (Lexington, Mass.: D. C. Heath & Co., 1974), chap. 3.

11. For one example of the application of a form of social studies of science to planning questions and a hint of the need for technological forecasting, see Qian Xuesen, "We Must Catch Up with and Surpass Advanced World Levels in Science and Technology within this Century," *Hongqi* 1977, no. 7 (July 4), in *SPRCM* 77–28. Also, it has recently been announced that new courses in "science organization and management planning" are to be offered at the new Haerbin University of Science and Technology and that the University of Science and Technology in Anhui will offer training in the management of scientific research. (Heilongjiang provincial service, April 28, 1978; NCNA dispatch, March 30, 1978.) See also Shen Hengyen, "A Comprehensive New Discipline: Futurology and the Study of the Future," *GMRB*, July 21–22, 1978, in Joint Publications Research Service, 72,188 and 72,041. Shen is affiliated with the Institute of Intelligence of the Academy of Social Sciences.

3: *PROFESSIONAL LIFE AND RESEARCH ADMINISTRATION*

1. For the U.S. see, for instance, William Kornhauser, *Scientists in Industry* (Berkeley and Los Angeles: University of California Press, 1962). For a fuller discussion of the bureaucratic-professional compromise in China, see Richard P. Suttmeier, *Research and Revolution* (Lexington, Mass.: D. C. Heath & Co., 1974), chaps. 3 and 4.

2. For a recent discussion of this question, see Peter Buck, "Western Science In Republican China: Ideology and Institution Building," in Arnold Thackray and Everett Mendelsohn, eds., *Science and Values: Pattern of Tradition and Change* (Atlantic Highlands, N.J.: Humanities Press, 1974), p. 163, passim. See also Danny Wynn Ye Kwok, *Scientism in Chinese Thought, 1900–1950* (New Haven: Yale University Press, 1965).

3. The general issue of culture and nationalism is treated masterfully in Joseph R. Levenson, *Confucian China and Its Modern Fate*, 3 vols. (Berkeley and Los Angeles: University of California Press, 1958–65; and idem, "Communist China in Time and Space: Roots and Rootlessness," *China Quarterly* 39 (July-September, 1969): 1–11. Discussions of nationalism and science and technology can be found in Ralph Croizier, *Traditional Medicine in Modern China* (Cambridge: Harvard University Press, 1968); Rensselaer W. Lee, III, "Ideology and Technical Innovation in Chinese Industry, 1949–1971," *Asian Survey* 12, no. 8 (August 1972): 647–61; and idem, "The Politics of Technology in Communist China," in Chalmers Johnson, ed., *Ideology and Politics in Contemporary China* (Seattle: University of Washington Press, 1973), 301–25.

4. See "A Great Debate on the Educational Front," *Peking Review* 1977, no. 51 (December 16): 4–9.

5. "New College Enrollment System," *Peking Review* 1977, no. 46 (November 11): 16–18.

6. Fang Yi, "On the Situation in China's Science and Education," *Peking Review* 1978, no. 2 (January 13): 17.

7. See Linda Mathews, "Abuse, Misuse Thin China Science Ranks," *Los Angeles Times*, November 12, 1978, p. 5.
8. NCNA dispatch, September 2, 1977.
9. NCNA dispatch, September 1, 1977.
10. See point 6 in Fang Yi, "Science and Education," p. 17.
11. See point 10 in ibid.
12. Ibid.
13. This discussion is based on Deng's speech as it appeared in *Peking Review* 1978, no. 12 (March 24).
14. OECD, *The Conditions for Success in Technological Innovations* (Paris: OECD, 1970), p. 56.
15. Shannon R. Brown, "Foreign Technology and Economic Growth," *Problems of Communism* 26 (July–August, 1977): 37. For a discussion of the administrative dimensions of technological innovation as a problem of science policy in China, see Richard P. Suttmeier, *Research and Revolution: Science Policy and Societal Change in China* (Lexington, Mass.: Lexington Books, 1974), chaps. 1 and 5.
16. Joseph S. Berliner, *The Innovation Decision in Soviet Industry* (Cambridge: MIT Press, 1976), pp. 8–18 and passim, cited in Brown, "Foreign Technology," p. 37. See also Joseph S. Berliner, "Bureaucratic Conservatism and Creativity in the Soviet Economy," in Fred W. Riggs, ed., *Frontiers of Development Administration* (Durham, N.C.: Duke University Press, 1970), pp. 569–600.
17. Thomas G. Rawski, "China's Industrial System," in U.S., Congress, Joint Economic Committee, ed., *China: A Reassessment of the Economy* (Washington, D.C.: Government Printing Office, 1975), pp. 181–98.
18. Suttmeier, *Research and Revolution*, chap. 5.

4: *MANPOWER AND EXPENDITURES*

1. These include Leo A. Orleans, *Professional Manpower and Education in Communist China* (Washington, D.C.: National Science Foundation, 1961); Chu-yuan Cheng, *Scientific and Engineering Manpower in Communist China, 1949–1963* (Washington, D.C.: National Science Foundation, 1965); and Yuan-li Wu and Robert B. Sheeks, *The Organization and Support of Scientific Research and Development in Mainland China* (New York: Praeger Publishers, 1970).
2. I am grateful to Jon Sigurdson for calling this report to my attention.
3. The 200,000 figure is one used in two recent works on the subject. Sigurdson estimated 200–300,000 (Jon Sigurdson, "Technology and Science in the People's Republic of China: An Introduction," unpublished paper, May 1978, p. 128). Swannack-Nunn estimated 100–200,000 in research and development (Susan Swannack-Nunn, *Directory of Scientific Research Institutes in the People's Republic of China* [Washington, D.C.: National Council for U.S.-China Trade, 1977], 1:9). Recently Zhou Peiyuan was quoted as saying that "China has only 400,000 scientists, engineers and technicians, but hopes to double their numbers

by 1985." Unfortunately, it is impossible to ascertain just what this figure represents. (See Linda Mathews, "Abuse, Misuse Thin China Science Ranks," *Los Angeles Times*, November 12, 1978, p. 5.)

4. Leo A. Orleans, "Research and Development in Communist China: Mood, Management, and Measurement," in U.S., Congress, Joint Economic Committee, ed., *An Economic Profile of Mainland China* (Washington, D.C.: Government Printing Office, 1967), pp. 549–78.

5. Leo A. Orleans, "Scientific and Technical Manpower," in OECD, ed., *Science and Technology in the People's Republic of China* (Paris: OECD, 1977), p. 99.

6. Cheng, *Manpower in Communist China*, p. 78.

7. Cf. Marianne Bastid-Bruguiere, "Higher Education in the People's Republic of China," in OECD, ed., *Science and Technology in the People's Republic of China*, table 6.1, p. 126.

   Bastid-Bruguiere's figures for 1966–67 may be too high since new enrollment dropped precipitously after 1960. According to a recent editorial in *RMRB*, new enrollments for the 1958–65 period were:

1958	265,000	1962	107,000
1959	270,000	1963	133,000
1960	320,000	1964	147,000
1961	169,000	1965	164,000

   The total enrollment in 1965 was some 670,000. ("Meticulously and Properly Carry out this Year's Enrollment Work for Institutions of Higher Education," *RMRB*, May 17, 1979, in *FBIS*, May 21, 1979.)

8. *Peking Review* 1979, no. 3 (January 19): p. 31. The figure for total enrollment is from "Meticulously and Properly Carry out this Year's Enrollment Work."

9. Cheng, *Manpower in Communist China*, pp. 118–23. This figure excludes 400 individuals who received doctorate or candidate degrees in the Soviet Union in the 1950s.

10. Orleans, "Scientific and Technical Manpower," p. 107.

11. Cheng, *Manpower in Communist China*, p. 123.

12. Orleans, "Scientific and Technical Manpower," p. 107.

13. Ibid.

14. NCNA dispatch, October 22, 1977, in *FBIS*, October 26, 1977.

15. Cheng, *Manpower in Communist China*, p. 54. Cheng offers a figure of 21,427 for this group, which is considerably higher than the 12,000 one would figure on the basis of 2,000 per year over six years.

16. NCNA dispatch, November 25, 1977, in *FBIS*, November 25, 1977.

17. Two thousand per year × ten years, minus 4,800.

18. 150,000 individuals over the course of eight years.

19. NCNA dispatch, July 15, 1978, in *FBIS*, June 20, 1978; NCNA dispatch, July 19, 1978, in *FBIS*, July 20, 1978. Cited in Pierre M. Perrolle, "Engineering Education in China: A Report On Observations of the U.S. Engineering Education Delegation to China, September 8–October 2, 1978" (Paper delivered at the Workshop on the Development of Industrial Science and Technology in the PRC:

Implications for U.S. Policy, St. George, Bermuda, January 3–7, 1979).

20. Sigurdson, "Technology and Science," p. 128.
21. Cf. Perrolle, "Engineering Education," p. 10.
22. Sigurdson, "Technology and Science," p. 110.
23. Ibid., pp. 111–16, especially p. 112.
24. Chu-yuan Cheng, cited in Bastid-Bruguiere, "Higher Education," p. 126.
25. Cheng, *Manpower in Communist China*, p. 78.
26. These institutions take their names from directives issued by Mao Zedong on May 7, 1966, and July 21, 1968.
27. Byung-joon Ahn. "China's Higher Education and Science in Flux," *Contemporary China* (March 1977): 22.
28. Boel Billgren and Jon Sigurdson, "An Estimate of Research and Development Expenditures in the People's Republic of China in 1973," Industry and Technology occasional paper no. 16 (Paris: OECD Development Center, July, 1977).
29. Orleans, "Research and Development," pp. 574–77.
30. Billgren and Sigurdson, "Research and Development Expenditures," p. 7.
31. Wu and Sheeks, *Research and Development in Mainland China*, p. 214.
32. Ibid., p. 214.
33. Beverly C. Rowen and Henry S. Rowen. "Japan's Security and Its Nuclear Future," unpublished final report prepared for the Energy Research and Development Administration, April, 1977. p. 48. The U.S. dollar figure is calculated using an exchange rate of 300 yen to the dollar.
34. At 2.03 *yuan* to the dollar.
35. The GNP estimate is from Arthur G. Ashbrook, Jr., "China: Economic Overview, 1975," in U.S., Congress, Joint Economic Committee, *China: A Reassessment of the Economy* (Washington, D.C.: Government Printing Office, 1975), p. 43.
36. Zhang Jingfu, "Report on the Final State of Accounts for 1978 and the Draft State Budget for 1979," *Peking Review* 1979, no. 29 (July 20, 1979): 17–24.
37. "Meticulously and Properly Carry out this Year's Enrollment Work."

5: INTERNATIONAL RELATIONS

1. Richard P. Suttmeier, "Recent Developments in the Politics of Chinese Science," *Asian Survey* 17, no. 4 (April, 1977): 381–83.
2. It is also true, however, that much of the technology Japan imported was considered obsolete by suppliers.
3. Yoshihiro Tsurumi, "Technology Transfer and Foreign Trade: The Case of Japan, 1950–1966" (Ph.D diss., Harvard University, 1968), cited in Ed McGaffigan and Paul Langer, *Science and Technology in Japan: A Brief Analytical Survey*, R-1736-ARPA (Santa Monica, Calif.: RAND Corporation, 1975), pp. 47–49.
4. Cf. Hans Heymann, Jr., "Acquisition and Diffusion of Technology in China," in U.S., Congress, Joint Economic Committee, ed., *China: A Reassessment of the*

Economy (Washington, D.C.: Government Printing Office, 1975), pp. 681, 704–7.

5. Nicholas R. Lardy, "The Impact of Technology Transfer on China's Domestic Economy" (Paper delivered at the Workshop on the Development of Industrial Science and Technology in the PRC: Implications for U.S. Policy, St. George, Bermuda, January 3–7, 1979).

6. *New York Times*, February 6, 1979.

7. Bohdan O. Szuprowicz, "China's Trade with Nonmarket Nations," *China Business Review* 5, no. 3 (May-June, 1978): 15.

8. Ibid., p. 13.

9. For instance, Nippon Steel and Nippon Kokan K.K. have agreed to train some 2,000 technical personnel from the Anshan steelworks in preparation for the planned doubling of Anshan's production capacity. (*Japan Economic Journal*, January 23, 1979.)

10. I am indebted to Hans Heymann for this example.

11. Susan Swannack-Nunn, *Directory of Scientific Research Institutes in the People's Republic of China* (Washington, D.C.: National Council for U.S.-China Trade, 1977), 1:5; and Robert Boorstin, *China's Professional and Industrial Societies* (Washington, D.C.: National Council for U.S.-China Trade, forthcoming).

12. NCNA dispatch, December 13, 1977, in *FBIS*, December 14, 1977.

13. NCNA dispatch, February 22, 1978, in *FBIS*, February 28, 1978.

14. "Making A Decision on Purchase of Foreign Technology," *China Business Review* 5, no. 3 (May-June, 1978): 9–11.

15. On the basis of information gathered during a recent trip to China on major procurement in nuclear physics, it is possible to infer that the process of exploring domestic capabilities probably involved not only the Institute of Oceanography, but also one of the CAS bureaus mentioned in chap. 2 and representatives of the Chinese shipbuilding and scientific instruments industries.

16. This hypothesis is a conjecture based on the fact that during an eighteen-part lecture series on "Scientific Experiment In A Great Revolutionary Movement" carried on Beijing Radio, the lecture on foreign technology issues was given by two individuals from these two institutes.

17. *China Business Review* 5, no. 3 (May-June, 1978): 59–63.

18. Agence France Presse (AFP) dispatch, Paris, January 21, 1978; and AFP dispatch, Hong Kong, January 21, 1978, in *FBIS*, January 23, 1978.

19. NCNA dispatch, April 11, 1978, in *FBIS*, April 12, 1978.

20. Dinah Lee, "China Looks for Trade Lift-off," *Far Eastern Economic Review*, April 28, 1978, p. 14.

21. *China Business Review* 5, no. 6 (November-December, 1978): 62.

22. *Peking Review* 1978, no. 25 (June 23): p. 30.

23. *China Business Review* 5, no. 6 (November-December, 1978): 64.

24. Kyodo dispatch, October 6, 1977, in *FBIS*, October 7, 1977; Kyodo dispatch, October 24, 1977, in *FBIS*, October 26, 1977.

25. Colin Lawson, "Overdraft: A New Word in Sino-German Trade," *Far Eastern Economic Review*, April 21, 1978. p. 40.

26. *New York Times*, July 23, 1978.

6: CHINESE SCIENCE AND SINO-AMERICAN RELATIONS

1. Representing the National Academies of Science and Engineering, the American Council of Learned Societies, and the Social Science Research Council.
2. Patricia Jones Tsuchitani, "Scientific Exchanges Between the United States and the People's Republic of China, 1972–1978" (unpublished paper, 1978).
3. *Chemical and Engineering News*, July 24, 1978; *New York Times*, July 15, 1978, p. 5; *Peking Review* 1978, no. 29 (July 21): 3–4.
4. *Peking Review* 1978, no. 29 (July 21): 3–4.
5. Ibid.
6. *Chemical and Engineering News*, July 24, 1978.
7. Of particular interest is the approval of the sale of an airborne infrared, multispectoral scanning device immediately after Zbigniev Brzezinski's visit to China in late May (*China Business Review* 5, no. 3 [May-June, 1978]: 45).
8. *Science*, June 30, 1978, p. 1,446. See also the contribution by Richard C. Lewontin and Richard Levins to the Op. Ed. page of the *New York Times*, July 23, 1978.

Index

Academic committees: and Chinese Academy of Sciences, 24

Academy of Sciences, *see* Chinese Academy of Sciences *and* U. S. Academy of Science

Academy of Traditional Chinese Medicine, 26

Agriculture: and four modernizations, 1–8 *passim*, 9; and Press mission, 85; and Sino-American cooperation, 86, 87, 99–100

All-China Federation of Scientific Societies, 28, 37

All-China Society for the Promotion of Scientific and Technical Knowledge, 28

Antielitism, 35

Antiprofessionalism, 35–36

Basic research, 47–48, 67, 76

Billgren, Boel: and science and technology expenditures, 62–63, 64, 65, 114

Branch academies, 24–25

Budget: and institutional reform, 19, 62–66

Capital construction, 65–66

CAS, *see* Chinese Academy of Sciences

Cheng, Chu-yuan: and scientific manpower, 56, 113

Chengdu University of Science and Technology, 23, 25

China: Japanese visitors to, 80, 115

China Metals Society, 74, 115

China National Machinery Import and Export Corporation, 75

China's New Invention Law, 104–7

Chinese Academy of Agricultural Sciences, 26

Chinese Academy of Sciences: and national work conference, 2–8 *passim*, 18, 20, 21; and new science system, 23–25, 39; and research administration, 43–44; and scientific manpower, 56–59 *passim*, 65, 66, 74, 75; and international cooperation, 78

Chinese Academy of Medical Sciences, 26

Chinese Academy of Military Science, 27

Chinese Academy of Social Sciences, 32

Chinese-American, *see* Sino-American

Chinese People's Political Consultative Conference (Dec., 1977), 18

Chinese science: and international relations, 41–42

Chinese trade: and nonmarket economies, 73

Coal production: and energy policy, 4

Committee on Scholarly Communication with PRC, 84, 116

Communication: and professional life, 39–40, 41

Computers, 4, 87

Confucianism, 35, 36, 41, 42, 111

Cooperation: and institutional reform, 19; and international scientific relations, 69, 86

Cultural revolution, 7, 11, 21, 27, 28; and professional life, 35–36, 36–42 *passim*;

Cultural revolution, (*cont.*)
and research administration, 42–43;
and scientific manpower, 62; and budget, 65; and international relations, 71;
and politics, 82; and the lost generation, 83, 109

Decision-making: and technology-transfers, 74–75, 76
Deng Xiaoping: and four modernizations doctrine, 1, 7, 12, 13, 16; and research administration, 45–47, 85, 86, 91

Eastern Europe: and Chinese scientific relations, 70
Economic development, 6–9 *passim*
Education, 7, 8; and institutional reform, 19; and Gang of Four, 37; and scientific manpower, 51–62; and modernization constraint, 66, 83
Eight-year plan: science and technology, 29, 30
Eleventh Party Congress, 2
Energy, 3–4, 77, 85; and Sino-American cooperation, 86, 87, 101–3
Engineers: and scientific manpower, 60–61
Environment, 77

Fang Yi, 3, 4, 5, 8; and Science and Technology Commission, 18; and offices held, 18, 19–23 *passim*, 28–29, 38, 43; and institutional constraints, 49–50; and scientific manpower, 52, 55, 56, 59, 61–62, 66, 78, 80, 85, 86, 98
Fifth National People's Congress (1978), 9, 109
Foreign consultancy arrangements, 76, 115
Foreign-training programs, 84
Forecasting: need in science and technology, 32
Four modernizations doctrine, 1; and scientific manpower, 6, 7, and constraints, 6–11 *passim*; and China's economy, 6, 8, 9; and expenditures, 65, 66; and international scientific relations, 72, 76, 79, 83, 84, 93
Fourth National People's Congress: "four modernizations" doctrine, 1

France and Chinese cooperative agreement, 77–78, 115
Frosch, Robert: and Chinese satellite-assembly facilities, 85, 116
Funding: and institutional constraint, 48

Gang of Four, 1, 2, 13, 14, 15, 16, 19; and professional life under, 37; and research administration, 45, 71, 75, 82, 83
Genetic engineering, 5, 6, 77, 78, 87, 115
Gradualism: and Sino-American relations, 89
Graduates: and scientific manpower, 53–59
Great Leap Forward, 24, 25, 35, 42, 43

Haerbin University of Science and Technology, 23, 25
Hefei University of Science and Technology, 25
Heilongjiang Engineering College, 23
High energy physics, 5, 10; and expenditures, 64–65; and cooperative projects, 69, 77; and policy planning, 88
Higher education institution: classification of, 25, 25–26
Hu Qiaomu, 13
Hu Yaobang, 13
Hua Guofeng, 2, 9–10, 11, 14, 15, 18, 46

ICSU, *see* International Council of Scientific Unions
Innovation: and institutional constraints, 48–50
Institute of Oceanography, and technology-imports, 48–50
Institutional constraints: and basic research, 47–48; and political support and funding, 48; and administrative capabilities, 48; and technological innovation, 48–50
Institutional reform, 18, 19
International Council of Scientific Unions, 69, 78, 79
International organizations: and scientific relations, 69
International scientific relations, 67; and technology-transfers, 68; and international organizations, 69; and commercial aspects of, 69, 76, 79, 87; and governmental aspects of, 69, 70, 76,

77–78, 79, 82–94; and professional aspects of, 69, 70, 79, 87; and the four modernizations, 72, 76, 79; and basic research, 76; and cooperative projects, 69, 86; and Sino-American relations, 82–94

International Union of Crystallography, 78–79

International Unions of Geological Sciences, Geodesy and Geophysics, 78–79

Japan: Chinese scientific relations with, 70–71; and technology-transfer, 75, 80–81, 90, 115

Japanese Overseas Economic Cooperation Fund: and Chinese use of, 72

Jiang Qing, 11. *See also* Gang of Four

Joint Commission on Scientific and Technological Cooperation, 86, 91, 92, 95–103

July 21 worker's college: and scientific manpower, 62

Laser technology, 4–5, 87

Liu Xiyao, 21, 80

Mao Zedong: and China's tasks, 2, 11, 12, 14–17 *passim*

Manpower: and four modernizations doctrine, 6, 7, 8, 109; and scientific development, 51–62; and foreign training, 59; and engineers, 60–61; and modernization constraint, 66

May 7 worker's college: and scientific manpower, 62

Medicinal plants, 78, 115

Meteorology: and Press mission, 85

Ministries of Machine Building, 27

Ministry of Agriculture, 26

Ministry of Civil Affairs, 52

Ministry of Defense, 26, 27

Ministry of Education, 25–26

Ministry of Foreign Trade, 75

Ministry of Public Health, 26

Ministry of the Metallurgical Industry, 74, 115

Missile program: and expenditure for, 64

Molecular biology, 10

Mutuality: and Sino-American relations, 88, 89

National Aeronautics and Space Administration, 85

National defense, 1, 8, 26

National Science Conference, 2, 3, 45, 52

Natural resources: and Press mission, 85

Nie Rougzhen, 20–21

Noninterference: and Sino-American relations, 89

Nuclear fuel cycle technology, 87, 88

Nuclear fusion: and expenditures, 66

Nuclear weapons program: and expenditure, 64, 65

Oceanography, 77, 85

Office of Science and Technology Policy: and Sino-American relations, 91, 93

Oil production: and energy policy, 3

Open information: and Sino-American relations, 88–89

Organization: and science and technology, 20–29

Orleans, Leo A: and scientific manpower report, 51, 52, 112

OSTP, *see* Office of Science and Technology Policy

"Outline Report," 13, 15, 52

Party leadership in science, 44–47

Planning: and science and technology organization, 29–33; and administrative capabilities, 48

Plant-tissue culture: and Beijing symposium, 78

Policy-analysis: and technology-transfers, 75, 88–93, 94; and Sino-American relations, 92–93

Political succession, 11–17

Politics, 11–17, 48, 83–84

Post-Cultural Revolution period, 27, 28, 29; and professional life, 37–42; and research administration, 43; and budget, 65; and international relations, 71; and the lost generation, 83

Post-Mao Zedong period: and budget, 65; and international scientific relations, 77; and manpower, 77; and government, 77–78, 84–86; and politics, 82–94

Pre-Cultural Revolution period, 19–21, 22–24 *passim*, 28–31 *passim*; and research administration, 42; and scien-

Pre-cultural Revolution period, (*cont.*) tific manpower in, 52–53, 54, 58, 61; and international relations, 70
Press, Frank: and China mission, 78, 84–86
Production Ministries, 26–27
Professional life, 34–42
Publicity: and institutional reform, 19

Qian Sangiang, 23
Qinghua University: and scientific manpower, 59

Research: and institutional reform, 18. *See also* Basic research
Research administration, 42–47
Responsibility: and institutional reform, 19
Rewards: and professional life, 39
Routinization: and Sino-American relations, 92

Science and technology: early approaches to, 1; and four modernizations doctrine, 1; and high priority for, 1–2, 11, 18; and institutional reform, 19; and organization, 20–29; and planning, 29–33, 88–93, 94; and expenditures for, 62–66; and international scientific relations, 68–69
Science and Technology Association, 19, 21, 28–29, 37
Science and Technology Commission, *see* State Science and Technology Commission
Science Planning Committee, 20
Scientific data bank development, 78, 115
Scientific manpower, *see* Manpower
Secretariat bureaus, 24
Seismology, 77
Shanghai Communique, 67, 99
Shanghai Machine Tools Plant, 27
Shanghai Petrochemical Works, 61
Sheeks, Robert B: and science and technology expenditures, 63, 64, 112, 114
Sigurdson, Jon: and scientific manpower, 52, 60, 112, 114; and science and technology expenditures, 62–63, 64, 65, 114

Sino-American scientific exchange, 84, 116
Sino-American scientific relations: and political aspects of, 82–94; and mutuality, 88; and open information, 88–89; and noninterference, 89; and gradualism, 89; and *n*th country awareness, 89–90, 91; and routinization of, 92; and the State Department, 92; and policy-analysis, 92–93; and science and technology cooperation, 95–98
Sino-American scientific exchange, 84, 116
Sino-American student exchange, 86
Soviet Union, 70
Space technology, 5; and expenditures, 64, 65; and cooperative projects, 69, 77, 85–87 *passim*, 100–101
State Council, 2, 20, 75
State Planning Commission, 21, 52
State Science and Technology Commission, 18, 20–23, 52
State Statistical Bureau, 52
State Technological Committee, 20
Student exchange, 88, 89, 98–99
Swannack-Nunn, Susan: and Chinese trading company consultants, 74, 115

Taiwan, 79
Technology-exports, *see* Technology-transfers
Technology-imports, *see* Technology-transfers
Technology-transfers: and Japanese example, 68–69, 73, 75; and payment for, 72, 74; and manpower shortage, 73, 74; and integration of, 73–74, 75, 76; and decision-making, 74–75, 76, 84; and Sino-American relations, 85, 116
Third-world countries: and Chinese scientific relations with, 71
Twelve-year plan: science and technology, 30–31

University of Science and Technology, 23, 58
U.S. Academy of Science, 85
U.S. Geological Survey, 85

Wages, 65
Wang Hongwen, 11–12. *See also* Gang of Four
Water conservation, 9
Western Europe: and Chinese scientific relations with, 70–71
West German Ministry of Research and Technology, 78
West German Science Exchange Center, 78
Wu, Yuan-li, 63, 64, 112, 114

Yang, C. N., 14, 40

Yao, Wenyuan, 11, 14. *See also* Gang of Four
Yu Guangyuan, 22
Yu Wen, 23

Zhang, Chunqiao, 11, 14. *See also* Gang of Four
Zhejiang University, 23, 25
Zhongshan University, 59
Zhou Enlai, 1, 11, 12, 14–17 *passim*, 71
Zhou Peiyuan, 14, 25